Thomas de Cantilupe

700 Years a Saint

St Thomas of Hereford

LOGASTON PRESS

FRONT COVER: St Thomas in reredos of Lady Chapel, Hereford Cathedral (Randoll Blacking, 1952). INSIDE FRONT COVER: The Life of St Thomas (1), fabric panels (2008) designed by Terry Hamaton, made by Croft Design (Much Wenlock). TITLE PAGE: St Thomas in stained glass at Munslow, Shropshire (fifteenth-century). INSIDE BACK COVER: The Life of St Thomas (2), *as above.* BACK COVER: St Thomas of Hereford, west window, Belmont Abbey

First published in 2020 by Logaston Press
The Holme, Church Road, Eardisley HR3 6NJ, UK
www.logastonpress.co.uk
An imprint of Fircone Books Ltd.

978-1-910839-41-6

Text © Michael Tavinor and Ian Bass, 2020; Essay (pp. 63–88) © Ian Bass, 2020.
Images © Hereford Cathedral/ Gordon Taylor, except: p. *viii* (top) © David Morrison, Chris Guy, Worcester Cathedral; p. 6 (l/h image) © United States House of Representatives; p. 6 (r/h image) © Becky Philips, Gloucester Cathedral; p. 7 © British Library; pp. 10–11 © Carol & Jim Kirby, Coleby, Lincs.; p. 19 (image no. 3) © Cressida Williams, Toby Huitson, Canterbury Cathedral; pp. 20–21 © Dominic Harbour; p. 27 (coin image) © Portable Antiquities Scheme/ South West Heritage Trust; p. 38 (top image) © Dan Terkla; p. 40 (l/h image) © Fabian Lochner; p. 53 © Ron Smith; p. 62 © Chris Green (Cambridge University)

Designed and typeset by Richard Wheeler.
Cover design by Richard Wheeler.

Printed and bound in Wales by Gomer

Logaston Press is committed to a sustainable future for our business, our readers and our planet. This book is made from paper certified by the Forest Stewardship Council.

British Library Catalogue in Publishing Data.
A CIP catalogue record for this book is available from the British Library.

CONTENTS

FOREWORD

At the heart of the story of Thomas de Cantilupe is a story of healing and redemption. Thomas, persecuted and excommunicated by Archbishop John Peckham, journeys to Italy, there to find absolution. The hurts of the past are healed and Thomas himself, through the miracles performed at his tomb, becomes a focus for Christ's healing.

The Right Revd Richard Frith,
bishop of Hereford 2014–19

The Right Revd Richard Jackson,
bishop of Hereford 2020

Thomas was the 45th bishop of Hereford and as the 105th and 106th bishops, we continue that long line of ministry, and look back in thanksgiving to those who have gone before us with the sign of faith. But we look forward too and pray that the great themes of Thomas's ministry – healing, redemption, faithfulness – may be marks of our ministry in the diocese today.

The Right Revd Richard Frith & The Right Revd Richard Jackson

ACKNOWLEDGEMENTS

The publication of this book has been made possible through the generous support of the 105th bishop of Hereford, the Right Revd Richard Frith, the Friends of Hereford Cathedral, and June and Leonard Chase. Michael particularly acknowledges with gratitude the support of an Ecclesiastical Bursary Award which enabled him to continue some of the work during a period of sabbatical study. Grateful thanks to the St George's Trust and the Friends of Hereford Cathedral for financial support. Canon Sandy Elliott has given valuable assistance regarding questions of design and layout, and Gordon Taylor has been unfailing in sourcing images of St Thomas for production. We also offer thanks to the Prior and community at Downside Abbey for their generosity in lending the skull of St Thomas for the duration of this festival year, and to Stonyhurst College for their continued trust in the cathedral as we care for the tibia of St Thomas. Further thanks to the Abbot and community of Belmont Abbey for their support of this project and for allowing us extensive use of images of stained glass from the Abbey Church. Ian gives gratitude to his parents, Keith and Margaret, who read the draft text with critical eyes.

Richard and Su Wheeler of Logaston Press have, as always, been such a support in bringing this book to publication. Both authors also wish to give grateful thanks to the cathedral community at Hereford, and especially to Canon Chris Pullin, Rosemary Firman, and Elizabeth Semper O'Keefe.

St Thomas of Hereford
All Saints Church, Hereford
(*by M.E. Aldrich Rope, 1952*)

INTRODUCTION

Hereford Cathedral is fortunate in having three saints or holy people who have nurtured its spirituality in the past and continue to do so in the present day. We have Ethelbert, our Saxon saint, acclaimed for his piety and martyrdom. We have Thomas de Cantilupe, our medieval saint, his sanctity proclaimed through records of miracles and after a complex canonisation process that lasted for more than 30 years. Finally, we have Thomas Traherne, our seventeenth-century priest, poet and writer – although not a saint in the official sense, since the Church of England has no process for such – numbered in the Church calendar of holy men and women. These three have been commemorated in recent years, with developments in the fabric of our cathedral – in wood, glass, stone and colour. Their stories are better known by the congregation and nurture our faith today, reminding us that we inherit a long and rich tradition, and that we are stewards of this tradition in our generation.

This year, 2020, we celebrate the 700th anniversary of the canonisation of St Thomas de Cantilupe. Perhaps not the most well-known of medieval English saints, he nevertheless holds a special place in their number:

- First, St Thomas of Hereford, as he is also known, is one of a number of bishops who were made saints in the thirteenth and fourteenth centuries, whose number include St Hugh of Lincoln (canonised, 1220), Edmund of Abingdon (canonised, 1246) and Richard of Chichester (canonised, 1262).
- Second, our St Thomas was canonised after a long enquiry held between London and Hereford from July to November 1307. The surviving documentation offers historians the longest extant process of canonisation of any medieval saint. The testimony contained within the surviving canonisation dossier offers 205 witness testimonies concerning his life, death and miracles, and demonstrates the patience and endurance of those who loved and recognised Thomas's holiness.
- Finally, there are surviving manuscripts which contain the medieval accounts of the miracles Thomas performed at the height of his cult, 1287–1312. The many miracles of healing recorded in these accounts mark out his curative

powers as second only to St Thomas of Canterbury in number and variety – a total of just over 460 by our St Thomas, compared to almost 650 by his namesake.

This year, 2020, we celebrate this remarkable man and his enduring place in Hereford's life. We also rejoice that we are part of a wider network of celebration for saints and pilgrimage in this festival year. Celebrations are being held for various reasons throughout the country:

- At Canterbury they are commemorating the 850th anniversary of the martyrdom of St Thomas Becket on 29 December 1170, and the 800th anniversary of the translation of his remains in 1220.
- At Lincoln there are events commemorating the 800th anniversary of the canonisation of St Hugh of Lincoln in 1220.
- At Bury St Edmunds they are celebrating their millennium, marking 1,000 years since King Cnut founded the abbey in 1020.
- At Salisbury, which celebrates the 800th year since its foundation stone was laid in 1220, and the cathedral's move from its original site at Old Sarum.
- It is a year, too, which has been marked by the Association of English Cathedrals, as the Year of Cathedrals and Pilgrimage.

Part of our particular celebrations at Hereford include the writing of this book, which draws out elements of our saint's life, as scholar, politician, bishop, healer and saint. There have been previous books concerned with St Thomas's life, death and miracles, not least the scholarly collection of essays produced for the 700th anniversary of his death in 1982, and the popular biography based on this by Gabriel Alington in 2001. Other books, journal articles – both popular and specialist – and documentaries have also been produced in recent years, highlighting St Thomas of Hereford's importance for study, and his enduring impact on both the medieval and modern life of Hereford Cathedral.

It is hoped that this book, with its many illustrations, will remind us all of his wonderful story and, more than that, will kindle in our hearts today the chief themes of St Thomas of Hereford's life: learning, integrity in political life, holiness, devotion to Christ, willingness to suffer for the sake of truth and an openness to the healing which Christ offers each of us.

We both hope that, through this book, St Thomas may become a little more 'real' to our generation and that his story may find a more valued place in the life of our cathedral, diocese and the wider Church.

Michael Tavinor, Dean of Hereford, and Ian Bass, New Year's Day 2020

The tomb of Walter de Cantilupe, bishop of Worcester 1236–66, in Worcester Cathedral

The visit of the Friends of Hereford Cathedral to Hambleden, Buckinghamshire, in August 2018, the 800th anniversary of Thomas's birth. The congregation – Anglicans and Roman Catholics – renewed their baptismal promises at the font in which Thomas was said to have been baptised in 1218

Cantilupe the Man

St Thomas of Hereford was born around the year 1218 at his father's manor of Hambleden, near Great Marlow in Buckinghamshire, and was baptised in the local village church there. He was descended on both sides from Anglo-Norman barons. His father, William, second baron de Cantilupe (d. 1251), held, like his father (William I, d. 1239) before him, the office of seneschal (steward) of the royal household of King John (1199–1216). Thomas's mother, Millicent (d. 1260), was the daughter of an Anglo-Norman lord, Hugh de Gournay, and had been first married to Amaury IV de Montfort, count of Évreux and earl of Gloucester (d. 1213). His uncle, Walter de Cantilupe, who became bishop of Worcester in 1236, was one of the most distinguished men of his time as both king's justice and bishop. Walter's influence brought Thomas into notable spheres of influence, not least of Robert Grosseteste, a learned and holy man who became bishop of Lincoln in 1235, and of William Raleigh, the likely patron or author of the legal text *On the Laws and Customs of the Kingdom of England* (*De Legibus et Consuetudinibus Angliae*), usually attributed to Henry de Bracton. He was also a close friend of Simon de Montfort, sixth earl of Leicester (d. 1265), whose cause in the Second Barons' War led to the first English Parliament in 1265.

Thomas was one of five brothers, the eldest of whom, William III de Cantilupe (d. 1254), married Eva de Briouze, an heiress of the Briouze family related to the great knight, William Marshal (d. 1219). Another brother, Hugh, became precentor of York and then archdeacon of Gloucester. Finally, his two younger brothers, John and Nicholas, became knights. Thomas also had three sisters, who all married into noble families, and Juliana, the one with whom he seems to have had the closest ties, was the wife of Marcher Lord, Robert II de Tregoz of Ewyas Harold (d. 1265).

Cantilupe the Scholar

Although a child, Thomas once expressed an ambition to be a soldier like his brothers. It was Bishop Walter of Worcester who took the young boy under his care and told him that he would follow in the footsteps of the great St Thomas of Canterbury, and would fight as a soldier of Christ. Thomas, like his brother Hugh, was destined for a career in the Church, and received his early education under the guidance of his uncle, Walter. In 1237, Thomas and Hugh were sent to begin their academical training at the University of Oxford, where Thomas's chief tutor was the Dominican, Robert Kilwardby who later became archbishop of Canterbury (1272–78). Not long after, sometime between 1237 and 1242, he and Hugh ventured to Paris to read the Arts. There they maintained a large household, in which they lived in almost princely style, with their own chaplain and tutor, and were even honoured by a visit from St Louis IX, the king of France (1226–70, canonised 1297).

By the mid-1240s, Thomas had taken his master's degree in Arts and next he embarked on a long course of legal studies, going first to Orleans, where he studied civil law under the noted thirteenth-century jurist, Master Guido de Guinis, and excelled in his studies. It was even said by the witnesses in 1307 that such was Thomas's depth of learning and ability that he was appointed by Master Guido to substitute for him on occasion. In about 1255, Thomas returned to Oxford to teach canon law, having been accepted as doctor in that faculty. In 1261 he was appointed as Chancellor of the university, an office then normally held for two years. During his tenure, Thomas won respect for the strictness and impartiality with which he maintained discipline among the large and unruly body of students, even managing to diffuse successfully a student riot which had broken out upon the visit of Prince Edward, future King Edward I (1272–1307), reportedly confiscating 20 bows and swords.

S. ȚHOM: IUS CHNONIC: OXON: DOCET

Thomas lectures in law at Oxford as Chancellor of the university, a post he held twice, first in 1261, then in 1273. *Belmont Abbey, west window*

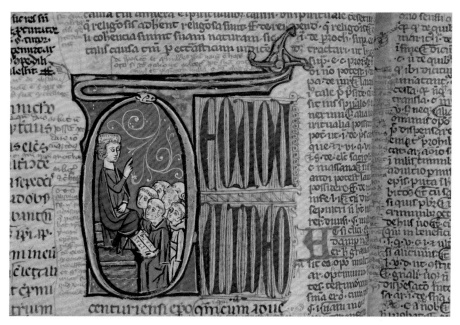

A master teaches a group of clerics. From a thirteenth-century canon law textbook made in Bologna. *Hereford, Hereford Cathedral Archives, MS o.8.2, fol. 59v*

The current Chancellor of the University of Oxford, Lord Patten of Barnes, gives the Cantilupe Lecture at Hereford Cathedral, October 2019

CANTILUPE THE POLITICIAN

IT WAS PROBABLY about 1263, when the dispute between King Henry III (1216–72) and his barons was drawing towards its crisis, that Thomas began to take part in political affairs. His sympathies, as might be expected, lay with the cause of Simon de Montfort, with which his uncle, Bishop Walter de Cantilupe, was so closely involved. In December 1263, having vacated the chancellorship of the University of Oxford, he went to Amiens as one of the representatives of the barons at the arbitration which St Louis had undertaken to make between them and King Henry. The issue largely turned on the barons' claim to a share in the choice of the king's counsellors, and Thomas was well qualified by his legal training to act as chief baronial proctor and to draft the three documents in which the baronial case was presented. There was little hope, however, that it would prevail and St Louis' verdict, given on 23 January 1264, supporting King Henry, led immediately to civil war. After Simon de Montfort's victory at the Battle of Lewes on 14 May 1264, a council of magnates was set up which ruled in the king's name. In February 1265 the council nominated Thomas, who was as acceptable to the king as anyone of his party could be, as chancellor of England and keeper of the king's seal. He held the great seal for only a very short time, handing it to Ralph of Sandwich on 7 May, but he retained the office of chancellor and exercised some of its functions until the defeat and death of de Montfort at the Battle of Evesham on 4 August 1265 brought the baronial government to an end.

During Thomas's time as Chancellor of England several exceptional events occurred which have been recorded in medieval governmental records. The first, on 7 March 1265, saw Thomas decline a writ issued by the Montfortian regime, refusing to seal it, the only recorded notice of such a thing happening during Henry III's reign. This was matched, according to one witness testimony in 1307, when Thomas likewise refused to seal a letter issued by the king, even going so far as to offer the royal seal back to him in an act of defiance.

Another exceptional instance occurs in the record of Thomas's appointment as Chancellor, which states that when the appointment was made 'the king with his own hand folded this writ and caused it to be sealed in his presence.' Finally, Thomas even changed the practice of 'giving' charters in the king's name, giving them instead under his own authority as Chancellor. This most remarkable of changes is evident in the text of copies of the 1265 Magna Carta in which the sealing clause states that Thomas 'gave' the charter.

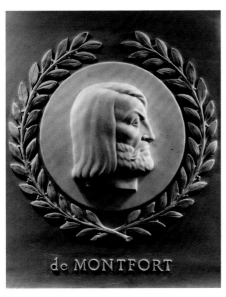

Simon de Montfort (sixth earl of Leicester) led the baronial opposition to the rule of King Henry III. After his victory at Lewes, he led the council (and thus the country, in effect) until his defeat and death at the Battle of Evesham in 1265. *One of 23 marble relief portraits in the US Capitol in Washington DC, with the inscription reading: 'established an early form of representative government in England'*

The coronation of King Henry III, 1216. Henry III appointed Thomas de Cantilupe as chancellor of the University of Oxford in 1261. Then, following Henry's defeat at the Battle of Lewes, Thomas was nominated by the Montfortian council of nine to be the Chancellor of England – confirming and sealing the enactments of the king and the council. He held this post from February until August 1265. *Stained glass, Gloucester Cathedral*

THOMAS DE CANTILUPE AND THE
DE MONTFORT MAGNA CARTA

Thomas's brief period as Chancellor of England in 1265 was associated with the second of Simon de Montfort's parliaments held between January and March 1265. This was the first parliament to which representatives of communities were summoned to Westminster, as well as barons, bishops and abbots. We see in that the birth of the House

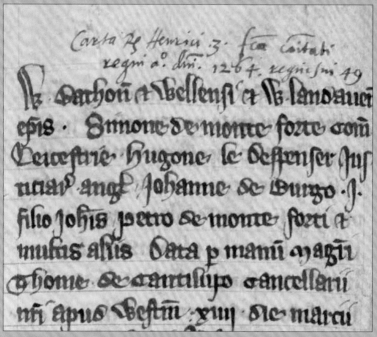

In 1265, Henry III was required to restate his oath to respect the Magna Carta of 1225. As Chancellor of England and keeper of the king's seal, Thomas was responsible for the writing and the sealing of all royal letters. The last three lines in the image above state 'given by the hand of Master Thomas de Cantilupe our Chancellor at Westminster on 14 March' (*Data per manum Magistri Thome de Cantilupo cancellarii nostri apud Westm' xiiij die Marcii. London, British Library, Cotton MS Claudius DII, fol. 128v*)

of Commons. During this parliament de Montfort made the captive Henry III reissue a slightly revised Magna Carta (to the advantage of the barons; for example, the level of fines payable for succeeding to titles or lands was reduced by a third as the word 'Marks' replaced 'Pounds'). Thomas was responsible for seeing that this revised Magna Carta was issued. Although none of the charters survive as such, the text can be found in other forms. In Hereford the main body of the text has been copied into Bishop Richard de Swinfield's Register, and it is tempting to think that this copy had been brought to Hereford by Thomas. In Henry III's official book copy (*inspeximus*) the complete text is given and we see that its conclusion contains these words: 'Given by the hand of Master Thomas de Cantilupe our Chancellor at Westminster …'.

An earlier bishop of Hereford, with connections to Magna Carta, Giles de Briouze was bishop of Hereford from 1200 to 1215. He had a difficult relationship with King John. His brother, William V de Briouze, and mother were infamously imprisoned by the king and starved to death in 1210, at the height of the king's dispute with Giles's father William IV. Giles went into exile in 1208 and returned in 1213, initially on better terms. However, following a dispute over a Briouze nephew's lands, King John confiscated some of the bishop's lands. Giles then joined the barons who opposed John, though by October 1215 he was reconciled and paid a fine of 9,000 marks to assure his episcopal possessions. *Tomb of Giles de Briouze in Hereford Cathedral, north choir aisle*

CANTILUPE THE PRIEST

IN 1245, THOMAS, accompanied by his elder brother, Hugh, his uncle, Walter, and his father, William II, attended the First Council of Lyons, where both Thomas and Hugh were appointed papal chaplains by Pope Innocent IV (1243–54). During the previous year, Thomas and Hugh had both received dispensations allowing them to hold benefices in plurality, a privilege of which Thomas would go on to make full, but scrupulous, use. Much of Thomas's ministry was exercised abroad while he was at university in Paris and Orleans. After his time as Chancellor of England, under the regime of Simon de Montfort, Thomas returned to his studies in Paris. His reconciliation with the king of England was made clear in the early 1270s when he returned in early 1272 to lecture at Oxford. He gained his doctorate in Theology in 1273. His reception in the church of the Dominicans was presided over by his old teacher and confessor, Robert Kilwardby, archbishop-elect of Canterbury, who spoke high praise of him, declaring 'that he never perceived him guilty of any mortal sin'. Soon after this, Thomas gained his second appointment as Chancellor of the University of Oxford, and it was during his second chancellorship that another student riot broke out. Thomas himself intervened bodily, in an attempt to make peace between the rioting northern and southern students, receiving a slash to his cloak by one overzealous sword-wielding northerner. Thomas's second term of office as chancellor was cut short when he attended the Second Council of Lyons in 1274, which had been convened by Pope Gregory X to end the schism between the Eastern and Western Churches. On this occasion the Cantilupian contingent comprised only Thomas and his nephew, William, the son of his brother Nicholas.

In England, Thomas received many ecclesiastical preferments. In addition to his prominent appointments as canon of Old St Paul's Cathedral, London, in 1264, archdeacon of Stafford and canon of Lichfield Cathedral in 1265, precentor and canon of York Minster in 1274, and canon of Hereford in the same year, he held many widely-scattered livings, largely acquired through family influence.

Among them were Winteringham (Lincolnshire), Deighton (Yorkshire), Bulwick (Northamptonshire), Sherborne St John (Hampshire) – the principal church at the heart of the lands of the St John family into which his sister, Agnes, had married – Coleby (Lincolnshire), Aston Cantlow (Warwickshire) – the principal seat of his own family's holdings – Hampton Lucy (Warwickshire), Dodderhill (Worcestershire), Bradwell (Essex), Ripple (Worcestershire) and Kempsey (Worcestershire). But Thomas was the most conscientious of pluralists, receiving papal dispensations for each additional benefice, which were later copied into the 1307 canonisation dossier. Thomas also took care to provide good and competent vicars, and also made frequent visits to his parishes, celebrating mass, preaching and hearing confessions, and gave generous alms to the poor and sick. He even used his wealth to repair and rebuild dilapidated church properties, and exercised his influence to protect the rights of his benefices.

Reports from the 1307 canonisation inquiry also note that Thomas entertained lavishly, maintained a respectable household, and remained extremely abstemious. He was known as a cultivated and social man. It is from the impression that Thomas made as canon of Old St Paul's Cathedral and the witness testimony of Brother Robert of St Martin, sacrist of St Bartholomew's Church, that we get the only description of Thomas's appearance. Brother Robert described

that 'he frequently heard [Thomas] preaching in that church and said that he preached very well and celebrated mass with great devotion, also that he had a face like an angel, which was amply bearded red and white, with a long nose – the hairs of his beard and head were part white and part red.' (*frequenter eum audivit predicantem in Ecclesia supradicta et dixit quod valde bene predicabat et multum devote celebrabat et habebat quasi vultum angelicum et erat albus et rubicundus bene barbatus, longo naso, et capilli barbe et capitis sui erant partim albi et partim rubrusi.*)

All Saints church, Coleby, in the diocese of Lincoln – one of the churches of which Thomas de Cantilupe was rector

All Saints, Coleby, in Lincoln diocese. Victorian stained glass depicting Thomas de Cantilupe

C: GEN: LVGDVNEN: I A D 1245

CANTILUPE THE BISHOP

ABOUT 1274, THOMAS, whose family had interests in Herefordshire, was appointed by John le Breton (bishop of Hereford 1269–75, himself a distinguished lawyer) to the prebend of Preston in Hereford Cathedral. It is reported in the 1307 inquiry that Thomas distinguished himself so much in his appointment that he became Bishop John's chosen candidate to succeed him, and was allowed to preach in the cathedral. In May 1275, Bishop John died, and Thomas was elected bishop by the canons on 15 June. Royal assent was signified a few days later. Thomas was consecrated as bishop of Hereford on 8 September 1275 at Canterbury by his former tutor, Archbishop Robert Kilwardby.

Thomas now became a favoured adviser to Edward I and regularly attended his councils, but he was chiefly occupied in the administration of his large and disordered diocese. He appears to have been assiduous in the encouragement of vocations, and, on 18 September 1277 at Leominster, ordained 35 sub-deacons, 36 deacons and 27 priests. He is known to have consecrated the Cistercian church at Abbey Dore in the early 1280s – protected by soldiers, as his right to do so was disputed by Bishop Thomas Bek of St Davids (1280–93).

As well as fulfilling his pastoral responsibilities with the utmost zeal and firmness, he gave careful attention to the management of the episcopal estate, especially his own palaces at Bosbury and Stretton Sugwas. He also devoted much of his energies to the defence of the rights and properties of his see against the encroachments of neighbouring lords, spiritual and temporal. One of his fiercest conflicts was with Gilbert de Clare, the 'red' earl of Gloucester (d. 1295), whom he forced to surrender his claim to the right of hunting on the episcopal chase on the western side of the Malvern Hills. It was said that, when Earl Gilbert had challenged Thomas regarding the court case whilst brandishing a writ claimed to be a royal postponement, Thomas retreated to a nearby wood

Opposite: In 1245, Thomas attended the First Council of Lyons, where he was appointed as a papal chaplain with his brother, Hugh. In 1244, Pope Innocent IV had given them the right to hold benefices in plurality. *West window, Belmont Abbey*

with his clergy. He soon re-emerged in full episcopal vestments, with his clergy at his back, hurling anathemas and excommunications at all who would impede the rights of the bishop of Hereford. Entries in his surviving bishop's register show that Earl Gilbert's foresters later came and sought absolution from Bishop Thomas for their wrongdoing. In another case, he caused the powerful Corbet family of Shropshire to make restitution to the bishopric, for estates taken from it in the Lydbury area. Thomas also oversaw Roger II de Clifford's (d. 1282) penance, imposed by the pope for Roger's role in the kidnap of Peter d'Aigueblanche, bishop of Hereford 1240–68, during the Second Barons' War. The penance caused Clifford to make pilgrimage barefoot to London, Canterbury and Hereford, the last three times, where Thomas thrashed Roger with birch twigs as he circulated the cathedral and cloister.

Thomas's relations with religious houses in the diocese were far from happy. When he thought that the townsfolk of Leominster were not receiving their due rights from the monks of the priory there he wrote, again and again, strongly urging that the monks make

Thomas de Cantilupe depicted in the east window of Pontesbury parish church, the chancel of which he consecrated in 1280

remedy. The people of the town used part of the priory church as their parish church, but the monks had been in the habit of closing the outer doors to protect their free access. This made for difficulties when the parish clergy needed access. The difficulty was not solved in Thomas's time and was met only when a separate chapel was, in later years, provided in the Forbury Chapel. In early 1279, Thomas made a visitation of the tiny house of nuns at Limebrook and greatly criticised the canonesses for their slack discipline. He wrote in similar vein to the canons of Chirbury and to those of Wormsley on comparable visitations. In one particular case from 1282, Thomas had to cite the subprior of Leominster, William de Winton, for his illicit affair in having seduced a nun from Limebrook.

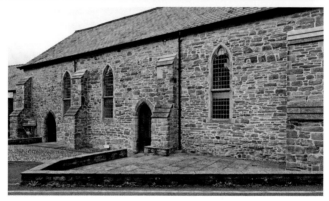

Top: The Cistercian Dore Abbey was consecrated by Thomas in the 1280s. It is said that he was protected by soldiers as his right to consecrate the church was disputed by Bishop Thomas Bek of St Davids, who had sent his vassal, and Bishop Thomas's nephew, John de Tregoz, to prevent the consecration from occurring

Above left: Wax cast of the episcopal seal of Bishop Thomas de Cantilupe, depicting him standing on a wolf, carrying his pastoral staff and raising his right hand in blessing. The field is embellished with groups of fleurs-de-lys in threes, a reference to his familial arms. Thomas is the first bishop of Hereford to have alluded to his coat of arms on his episcopal seal

Above right: While bishop of Hereford, Thomas had written repeatedly to the Benedictine monks at Leominster Priory, especially regarding the monks not sharing their building with the local people. This issue was unresolved when Thomas died in 1282, but, in that same year, Archbishop John Peckham founded the Forbury Chapel, dedicated to St Thomas Becket and built with the permission of Thomas's successor, Bishop Richard de Swinfield

CANTILUPE THE 'WHITE MARTYR'

IN 1279 ARCHBISHOP Robert Kilwardby was succeeded as archbishop of Canterbury by John Peckham (1279–92) who, like his predecessor, had once been Thomas's teacher. But he and Thomas were opposed by temperament and training, and a bitter quarrel soon arose between them. The first signs of tensions between the two prelates came in Bishop Thomas's criticism of Archbishop John's handling of his dispute with the bishop of St Asaph. The first, earnest demonstration of soured relations is clear when, in 1279, while Bishop Thomas was absent overseas, the chapter of Hereford became embroiled in a matrimonial suit. An appeal was made by the husband direct to the court at Canterbury, without reference to the bishop's court at Hereford. The delegate of the dean's court in Hereford disregarded prohibitions from the archiepiscopal court and continued regardless, resulting in threats of excommunication and interdict. Bishop Thomas spent this time in Normandy, where he stayed at the Benedictine Abbey of Lyre, in Évreux, which has close links with Herefordshire. Soon after Bishop Thomas's return from Normandy the major quarrel which would force him to visit the pope in Italy began.

The quarrel between Bishop Thomas and Archbishop John ignited in late 1280, and is primarily concerned with the complexities inherent in thirteenth-century English diocesan governance. At its core, the dispute began when Bishop Thomas's official refused to cite the executors of two Hereford canons before Canterbury's Court of Arches, since they owned property in more than one English diocese. Where Archbishop John had expanded the purview of the Court of Arches and felt that it was an archiepiscopal matter, Bishop Thomas insisted that the probate of the canons' wills should come, instead, before the diocesan court of Hereford. At the time that this dispute began, Bishop Thomas was in Normandy, returning only in autumn 1281.

Archbishop John pursued his feud with Bishop Thomas with great zeal, describing him as a man 'who excogitated malice under the demeanour of a dove'. The dispute came to a head in early 1282 when Archbishop John demanded Bishop Thomas excommunicate his official who had ignored archiepiscopal authority. Bishop Thomas's stubborn support of the court of Hereford and his official, in resisting what he felt to be an infringement of his rights, finally brought excommunication upon him. Convinced of the injustice of this treatment and with the support of the king and wise friends, Thomas decided to travel to Rome to appeal for papal intervention.

This momentous journey began on 9 March 1282. The expenditure for each day was carefully recorded in the household roll, but, as the party passed through 11 different currency zones, it is uncertain how much was actually spent. Thomas and his retinue crossed the Channel from Dover to Boulogne, and arrived in Paris on 21 March. They followed rivers and roads through France, and in Italy they followed the coastal routes. The average distance was 20 miles a day, sometimes considerably less.

Bishop Thomas was ill when the party reached Florence on 14 May 1282. He rested and sent two of his clergy to speak for him at the curia which, with the papal residence, had moved away from Rome. The pope, Martin IV (1281–85), appointed two cardinals to investigate the case and they pronounced Bishop Thomas to be of fit and proper status to be admitted to the papal curia which was then based at Orvieto. Thomas, partially recovered, was greeted warmly by the pope, but by this time he was thin and worn out from the travelling and strain. Nevertheless, throughout July, he continued to visit the curia (now at Montefiascone, Tuscany) two or three times a week for hearings of his case. He became seriously ill in August and was visited in his lodgings, Castrum Florenti at Ferento, by Pope Martin IV on 14 August. He managed to celebrate mass, made his will and was later given absolution by a papal penitentiary. He died at Castrum Florenti on 25 August 1282.

Thomas's body lay exposed for six days, emitting a 'heavenly fragrance'. His heart was removed and the rest of the body boiled to separate the flesh from the bones. His flesh was interred inside the monastery of San Severo – near the wall of the south doorway used by the canons to enter the church from the cloister – and the Mass was attended by five cardinals, indicating the respect Thomas had earned. It was conducted by Cardinal Girolamo Masci, the future Pope Nicholas IV (1288–92). It was also said by one Worcestershire annalist that the place where the liquid Thomas in which had been boiled was poured, soon welled up into a holy, miraculous, spring.

Thomas de Cantilupe is often compared to Thomas Becket, whom he greatly revered. Certainly there are many resonances between the two saints – in iconography, in the stories of their respective miracles, in their liturgies. However, while Becket was 'fast-tracked' to sainthood in three years, it took 38 years for Cantilupe to achieve that status; and while Becket is seen as a 'red martyr' who shed his blood for Christ, Cantilupe is hailed as a 'white martyr': one who suffered for Christ (not least through his persecution by Archbishop John) – though not to the extent of that shedding of blood.

Above: Bishop Thomas in dispute with Archbishop John.
Hereford Cathedral hangings in the north transept

Opposite: **1.** Thomas arrives at the papal court and is welcomed by Pope Martin IV. *West window, Belmont Abbey.* **2.** Thomas dies at Castrum Florenti on 25 August 1282. *West window, Belmont Abbey.* **3.** Tomb of Archbishop John Peckham, in the north transept of Canterbury Cathedral. **4.** The household roll detailing every stage of the journey, with provisions obtained, during Thomas's fateful journey of March–August 1282. Here we see the end of the roll from 7 April, when he was in Brioude (France), to his arrival in Montefiascone on 6 August. *Hereford, Hereford Cathedral Archives, R745*

1

2

3

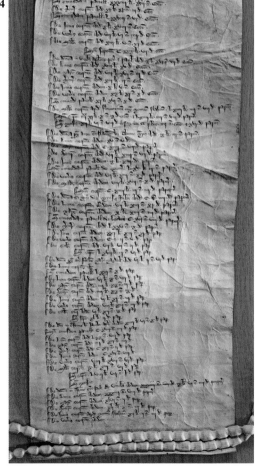

4

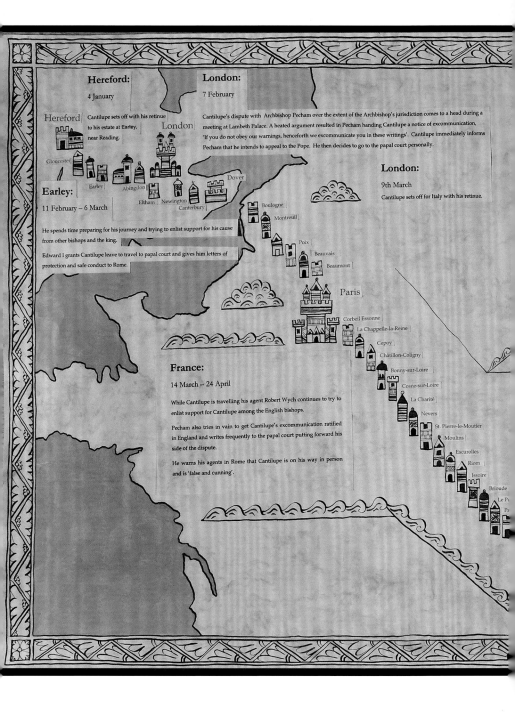

Hereford:

4 January

Hereford — Cantilupe sets off with his retinue to his estate at Earley, near Reading.

Gloucester

London:

7 February

London — Cantilupe's dispute with Archbishop Pecham over the extent of the Archbishop's jurisdiction comes to a head during a meeting at Lambeth Palace. A heated argument resulted in Pecham handing Cantilupe a notice of excommunication, 'If you do not obey our warnings, henceforth we excommunicate you in these writings'. Cantilupe immediately informs Pecham that he intends to appeal to the Pope. He then decides to go to the papal court personally.

Earley:

Earley Abingdon

Eltham Newington

11 February – 6 March

Canterbury

Dover

He spends time preparing for his journey and trying to enlist support for his cause from other bishops and the king.

Edward I grants Cantilupe leave to travel to papal court and gives him letters of protection and safe conduct to Rome.

Boulogne

Montreuil

Poix

Beauvais

Beaumont

Paris

Corbeil Essonne

La Chappelle-la-Reine

Cepoy

Châtillon-Coligny

Bonny-sur-Loire

Cosne-sur-Loire

La Charité

Nevers

St. Pierre-le-Moutier

Moulins

Escurolles

Riom

Issoire

Brioude

Le Pt

Pr

London:

9th March

Cantilupe sets off for Italy with his retinue.

France:

14 March – 24 April

While Cantilupe is travelling his agent Robert Wych continues to try to enlist support for Cantilupe among the English bishops.

Pecham also tries in vain to get Cantilupe's excommunication ratified in England and writes frequently to the papal court putting forward his side of the dispute.

He warns his agents in Rome that Cantilupe is on his way in person and is 'false and cunning'.

The Last Journey of
THOMAS CANTILUPE
4th January ~ 25th August 1282

Florence:

14 May

Cantilupe is delayed by illness. He sends three of his companions ahead to the papal court at Orvieto where they argue that Cantilupe's excommunication is not legal.

In early June the cardinals decide that Cantilupe is 'a man of fit and proper status and, as such, ought to be admitted' to the court.

10 June

Cantilupe arrives at court of Pope Martin IV at Orvieto to pursue his appeal personally.

4 July

The papal court moves to Montefiascone.

Cantilupe stays nearby at Ferento and attends the court several times to continue his appeal.

25 August

Cantilupe dies at Ferento. His flesh is buried at San Severo, Orvieto.

His heart and bones are returned to England, his heart being sent to a college of canons at Ashridge, the bones being interred at Hereford.

Genoa

Florence

Rome

The last journey of Thomas de Cantilupe, 4 January–25 August 1282 (*Dominic Harbour, 2005*)

The Benedictine monastery turned Premonstratensian house of San Severo (now a hotel called La Badia) where Thomas's body was boiled, seen from the city walls of Orvieto

Thomas's remains were returned to England, and his heart, encased in lead, entrusted to a community of Bonhommes at Ashridge in Hertfordshire, founded in 1283 by Edmund, second earl of Cornwall. The monastic buildings were destroyed at the Dissolution, and the present house constructed between 1808 and 1814. A statue of Thomas, in episcopal vestments, can be seen on the grand staircase of the house

Cantilupe the Healer

B ishop Thomas's bones were brought from Italy to the harbours of France by the Herefordian household which had accompanied him on his final journey. His bones and heart had been entrusted to his accountant, John de Clare. On hearing of Thomas's death, Archbishop John maintained that he was excommunicate and would not allow his bones entry back into England. The Herefordian contingent disregarded the archbishop's threats, however, bringing the bones back to England and deliberately walking through archiepiscopal lands where it was reported that the casket containing them emitted blood. At the behest of Edmund of Almain, second earl of Cornwall (1272–1300), at the Council of Northampton in January 1283, Bishop Thomas's bones were absolved of their excommunication. His heart was given to Edmund and deposited at his new monastic foundation at Ashridge in Hertfordshire. His bones were laid to rest in his cathedral, at Hereford, before the altar of the Virgin Mary in the Lady Chapel.

Bishop Richard de Swinfield, Thomas's successor to the see of Hereford, had been a member of Thomas's household for 18 years, and revered his master. He saw it as his duty to drive the campaign for Thomas's canonisation based on his holiness. It was no easy task. Inquiries began in 1286, when Bishop Richard appointed men to go to the monastery of San Severo and report whether any miracles had been performed at the holy spring which had erupted at the site where Thomas's flesh and viscera had been poured. A year later, Thomas's miraculous career as a holy healer was to begin.

On Maundy Thursday, 3 April 1287, Thomas's bones were removed from the Lady Chapel and laid in an altar-type tomb which had been constructed for him in the north transept. Not long before that, the first miracle of healing had taken place. On Palm Sunday 1287, Edith, the wife of Robert the Ironmonger, had been reported as mad and brought to the cathedral. She had apparently lashed out, biting her mother on the finger or nose, attacked her husband, and had blasphemed against God. Edith was brought to the cathedral and was in the area where Thomas's remains were being stored before their translation to the north transept, when she reportedly had a vision of him in episcopal vestments and was cured. It was by rapid word of mouth that the news of this miracle spread, against Archbishop John's orders to suppress the stories, and people flocked to Hereford from the nearby area and later from further afield. On the day of translation on Maundy Thursday several miracles were reported and the cult was soon in full swing. While the popularity of Thomas's cult was short-lived (miracles stopped being recorded in 1312, though there is one final miracle dated to 1404), more than 460 miracles were recorded by the tomb's custodians between 1287 and 1312.

The miracles reported and recorded reflect a huge range of healing incidents: the blind received sight, the lame made to walk, the demented restored to reason. A large proportion of the miracles are of resurrection after apparent death by accidents of drowning or smothering, and even execution by hanging. Many of the miracles also involve children: a Tewkesbury boy 'died' in a cask of beer and a London child drowned in a rain barrel by the hall door – Thomas effected their resuscitations. There are many other stories, too, such as of a wine ship from Gascony, which was caught in a storm in the Irish Sea. After her Bristol master advised the crew to pray to Thomas at Hereford, the storm abated. Thomas's powers also extended to animals as well. Several knights reported their falcons which had been injured or died. When they bent silver pennies over them and dedicated the coins to Thomas, the animals often recovered. The accounts of the state of the sick and bereaved who came to the shrine throw a brilliant light upon conditions of ordinary life in these times.

Pilgrimage resulted in the cathedral gaining much money and being able to embark on a scheme of rebuilding which can still be seen: the north porch with its depictions of pilgrims and others; the effigies of the former bishops of Hereford lining the north and south choir aisles; and the central tower with its distinctive ballflower decoration. This was funded from the donations left at Thomas's tomb-shrine in the north transept. During the 1307 canonisation inquiry in Hereford, an inventory was made of the non-monetary offerings at the shrine at the start, and again at the end. In total the record made in August accounted:

Inventory of non-monetary offerings made at the shrine of Thomas de Cantilupe (1307)

170 ships in silver and 41 in wax.

129 silver images of whole and diverse body parts.

436 wax images of people.

1,200 wax images of body parts.

77 figures of horses, animals and birds.

An uncountable multitude of wax images of eyes, breasts, teeth, and ears.

95 silk and linen garments.

108 sticks used by cripples.

3 carts used to transport infirm pilgrims and 1 in wax.

10 large square candles.

38 cloths made from gold thread and silk.

Many belts.

A great quantity of jewellery including: 450 gold rings, 70 silver rings, 65 gold brooches, 31 silver brooches, and many diverse gemstones.

And other items including chains off ships brought by prisoners, anchors of ships, and lances, arrows, and many swords and knives.

In November, when the inventory was made again, they accounted another wax and two silver ships, another silver image of a person, 85 more wax images of body parts, and two more garments of clothing. While the commissioners did not make accounts of money left at the shrine, they made a final note of seeing innumerable numbers of candles which had been deposited as votive offerings.

1. Bishop Richard de Swinfield, Thomas's successor as bishop is cured of gall stones after drinking wine in which a relic of Thomas had been dipped. 2. A man is held in prison and was so heavily chained that his arms were broken. He prays to Thomas for deliverance, promising to make a pilgrimage to the tomb. Duly released and cured, he promptly forgets his pledge and consequently finds himself back in his chains. Given another chance he makes the pilgrimage! 3. A knight lights a candle at the shrine. 4. A cripple approaches the shrine. 5. A woman gives thanks for the restoration to life of her sick child. 6. A woman prays at the shrine for the cure of her sick child (*Belmont*)

26

Wax images of parts of the body cured by the saint were offered at the shrine. Here we see a pilgrim offering a replica of his cured leg – as seen in the St William window at York Minster

Pilgrims at the tomb – an artist's impression by Robert Byron. Sometimes, coins were 'bent' over the ill or dead to effect a miracle. This was noted in the 1307 canonisation inquiry to be an 'English custom'

A bent penny of the reign of Edward I, of the type that may have been used in intercession to Cantilupe *Portable Antiquities Scheme (PAS) DEV-8F79AE*

THE STORY OF WILLIAM CRAGH

In December 1290, an unlikely group of pilgrims set off from Swansea for the tombshrine of Thomas de Cantilupe at Hereford Cathedral. Among them was William Cragh, also known as William ap Rhys, a Welsh outlaw, walking barefoot and wearing a noose around his neck.

Just a few weeks before, Cragh had faced Anglo-Norman baronial justice after being captured and convicted for his role in the burning of the Briouze residence of Oystermouth Castle, and for his part in the rebellion of Rhys ap Maredudd. In November 1290 Cragh was hanged on Gibbet Hill in Swansea. The hanging did not go to plan. Before being hanged, Cragh bent a silver penny and requested Thomas de Cantilupe to take pity on him so that he might do penance for his wrongdoings on earth. According to the contemporary account, when they first hoisted him on the gallows, the rope with which he was to be hanged, snapped. On the second attempt the transverse beam of the gallows broke. Finally, on the third time, they succeeded and hanged him until he was dead. Later, when his family were burying him and he was placed in the grave, Cragh suddenly sat up and professed that Thomas de Cantilupe had seen fit to grant him life. Now, William Cragh travelled together with his executioners to give thanks at the tomb of the putative saint, with William de Briouze even having a wax figure of a man on a gallows made as an offering.

In association with the University of Southampton, Hereford Cathedral helped establish the St Thomas Way, a route from Swansea to Hereford, tracing the steps of William Cragh and the places he visited on his pilgrimage *http://thomasway.ac.uk/*

RICHARD DE SWINFIELD (d. 1317)

RICHARD DE SWINFIELD's last name may indicate his birth at Swingfield located near Folkestone, Kent. By 1264, he was a member of the household of Thomas de Cantilupe, a role he continued for 18 years as Thomas's chaplain, secretary, agent, friend and constant companion. As with many clergy of his day, he held a multiplicity of ecclesiastical preferments, as archdeacon of London, archdeacon of Shrewsbury and prebendary of Hereford. Richard de Swinfield became bishop of Hereford in 1283. During his episcopate, he was not as involved in politics, and spent most of his time in his diocese. He rarely attended parliament and synod, usually excusing himself on the grounds of urgent diocesan business or his own bad health.

Bishop Richard was concerned to make sure that his clergy were well treated. He worked to ensure that churches within his diocese were served by the best-trained clergy, and was vigilant over monastic houses. His main efforts, though, went toward securing the canonisation of his predecessor Thomas de Cantilupe. For this he worked tirelessly, contacting cardinals, bishops and successive kings. Despite his persistence, however, the canonisation of his master did not take place until 1320, three years after Bishop Richard's death, on 15 March 1317.

Three of his nephews were given positions within the cathedral, with Gilbert becoming chancellor in 1287, John becoming archdeacon of Shrewsbury in 1289, treasurer in 1293 and finally being appointed as precentor in 1294, and Richard who was appointed as a canon in 1294.

A record of Bishop Richard's expenses has survived for the years 1289 and 1290. The accounts offer a rare glimpse of the organisation and expenses of a major household of that period. During the 296 days covered by the record, his household moved 81 times, with 38 of these stops associated with a visit to his diocese during April to June.

Above: Bishop Richard de Swinfield's tomb, in original form, as depicted by Dugdale (*1684*).
Below left: A detail of the canopy above Bishop Richard's tomb in Hereford Cathedral.
Below right: The gilded wooden head of Bishop Richard's crosier – his staff of office – shows the Blessed Virgin Mary carrying the Christ child, with Christ enthroned on the other side

Above: Detail of the tomb of John de Swinfield (precentor 1294–1311), nephew to Bishop Richard de Swinfield, with its rebus or pun on the Swinfield name, a line of pigs running over the arch, each bearing the heraldic arms of the cathedral. *Below*: Bishop Richard's private paten and chalice were found in his tomb just to the right of his head. Both were made of sterling silver in the mid-thirteenth century, the paten inscribed with the words 'Dextera Dei' [the right hand of God] with an image of God's right hand raised in blessing

CANTILUPE THE SAINT

In 1290, Richard de Swinfield, Thomas's successor as bishop, appealed to Pope Nicholas IV to consider canonising his predecessor, and this request was followed in the next few years by appeals from King Edward I, the archbishop of York, fifteen other bishops, seven abbots, eleven earls and numerous barons and noblemen who wrote proclaiming Thomas's virtues and miraculous powers. Finally, on 23 August 1306, Pope Clement V (1305–14) issued a papal bull authorising a canonisation inquiry to take place in 1307, to investigate Thomas's life, death and reputed miracles.

In 1307, the three papal commissioners embarked on a process of enquiry, conducted in Hereford and London between July and November. Their enquiry interviewed those who had known Thomas personally or had claimed his miraculous intervention in their favour. The evidence includes testimony on Thomas's life and miracles, lists of the miracles arranged both in chronological order and according to type, and inventories of offerings at the shrine. The inquiry in London ran for four weeks, from 13 July until 12 August, after which the commissioners turned to Hereford, where the enquiry concluded on 12 November.

For all the rigour of the enquiry, canonisation was still not granted immediately. It must have seemed as if Thomas's cause, like that of other saintly bishops who were candidates for canonisation in those times – such as Robert Grosseteste of Lincoln, Walter de Suffield of Norwich, and Thomas's own uncle, Bishop Walter of Worcester – would come to nothing. Indeed, Bishop Richard died in 1317 without seeing the successful conclusion of his life's work. He was succeeded by Adam Orleton (1317–27) who continued the process, even getting King Edward II to write to the pope urging the canonisation.

Eventually, on Thursday 17 April 1320, Pope John XXII (1316–34) went to the Cathedral church of Notre Dame des Doms in Avignon and, with his brother cardinals, proceeded to canonise Thomas. The pope preached on the text: 'He was tried and found perfect and he shall be in glory'. (*Sirach 31: 10*).

From the Bull of Pope John XXII for the canonisation of Thomas de Cantilupe:

At length the saint, from being an innocent lamb, was made a good shepherd in the church of Hereford, and ever studying to advance from virtue to virtue from the time when he was placed in so high a position in the temple of God, so shone as to be called the very jewel of bishops.

He went before his sheep to the pastures, defended them from fierce wolves and led them back to Christ's sheepfolds, fed them by word and example. He stoutly defended the rights of his church, having put on justice as a breast-plate. Thus this blessed man, in committing his soul to God, from being a stranger and pilgrim became an illustrious citizen of heaven.

A notarial instrument (*Hereford, Hereford Cathedral Archives 1445*) – a document recording the *inspeximus* in the presence of Adam Orleton, bishop of Hereford, of the original papal bull of Pope John XXII for the canonisation of Thomas de Cantilupe in 1320. The text of the original document is recited, setting out Cantilupe's excellent character, his abstinence and learning, and describes a few of the miracles attributed to him

ENGLAND'S TWO THOMASES: CANTILUPE AND BECKET

It is hard not to make comparisons between St Thomas of Hereford and St Thomas of Canterbury, and their respective reputations. Both held the office of Chancellor of the realm, both quarrelled with barons and lords, both disagreed with the policies of a king named Henry, both took self-imposed exile in Normandy, both wore hair shirts, and both were the centre of major cults performing hundreds of miracles. This barely scratches the surface of their similarities, yet there were differences, such as their placement in the Church hierarchy, and where their cults operated. These comparisons were certainly also known to the medieval clergy in the diocese of Hereford. In one tale, Bishop Walter of Worcester was said to have told his young nephew, upon hearing Thomas's wishes to become a knight like his brothers, that he would follow in the footsteps of his namesake as a soldier of Christ.

St Thomas of Hereford's cult was very much moulded on that of his namesake. Imagery at the shrine in the north transept of Hereford Cathedral, placed the prelates near to each other in wall paintings, and elsewhere in stained glass windows. Likewise, scholars have theorised that the Limoges reliquary chasse in the cathedral special collections would have been displayed in the south transept of the cathedral (though the evidence for this location is uncertain), offering a pilgrimage route around the cathedral, and to both Thomases. Texts containing the offices for the cathedral's services compared the prelates, declaring that Becket 'underwent the punishment of the sword' while Cantilupe 'achieved martyrdom in his heart'. Later funerary monuments, such as that of Peter, Lord Grandison, and Archdeacon Richard Rudhale, display Cantilupe and Becket together. At the cathedral's own charitable foundation of St Katherine's Hospital, Ledbury, distinction was made in a list of relics compiled in 1316 between 'the oils of St Thomas with other minute items' and 'items of the blood, hair and vestment of the blessed Thomas the martyr'. Further afield, a stained glass window at Credenhill church, dated to c.1306, displays the two prelates together – their shared name in the centre of the inscription. The glass commissioned by Bishop Thomas Spofford (1421–48) for his episcopal palace at Stretton Sugwas, also displayed the two prelates near each another. Finally, some medieval bishops, such as Hamo Hethe of Rochester (1319–52), sent several penitents from his diocese to both Cantilupe's shrine in Hereford and Becket's shrine in Canterbury.

Opposite: When Thomas was proclaimed a saint in 1320 some of the texts directed to be used on his feast day were exactly those already in use for Becket. Clearly, in life and in death, the two Thomases, Cantilupe and Becket, had many similarities. Credenhill's window was once thought to mark the centenary of the canonisation but is now thought to date from c.1306, before Cantilupe was proclaimed a saint

Tomb of Peter, Lord Grandison (d. 1358). Grandison's image, with its 1350s-style armour, and restored imagery of the saints of Hereford above, from left to right: Thomas de Cantilupe, Ethelbert, John the Baptist, Thomas Becket, flanking the Coronation of the Virgin. The tomb occupies an important position opposite the newly established shrine of St Thomas, whose relics were translated here in 1349, the year of the Black Death

Hereford Cathedral once had a wealth of monumental brasses, many of which have perished. This brass to Ethelbert remains. It was originally placed within the shrine of St Thomas of Hereford, reminding all of the close link between the two saints. Ethelbert is shown seated, holding his severed head. The funerary brass commissioned for Thomas's monument is known to be one of the earliest in England, and certainly the earliest for a bishop

Translation of St Thomas

O N 25 October 1349, the relics of St Thomas of Hereford were translated to a new shrine in the Lady Chapel, in the presence of King Edward III (1327–77) and Queen Philippa. The Black Death was raging, a huge number of Hereford clergy died, and John de Trillek, bishop of Hereford (1344–61), ordered the translation partly as a means of seeking God's mercy and help. Pilgrims continued to come to Hereford. Although reduced in numbers, they provided funding for the embellishment of the new shrine. It was this Lady Chapel shrine that the Reformers destroyed, most likely at the end of the 1540s. Hereford was a long way out and nowhere near as high profile as Canterbury. But the 1287 tomb-shrine, where all the miracles had occurred, still stood. The Reformers, having done their work in the Lady chapel, presumably forgot about this, so the original tomb remained unscathed and today stands as one of the few medieval saints' shrines to have survived.

Thomas's remains are translated to a new shrine in the Lady Chapel in the presence of King Edward III and Queen Philippa. *West window, Belmont Abbey*

Some scholars believe that, for some of its early history, the Hereford Mappa Mundi hung near to the tomb-shrine in the north transept. Pilgrims coming to see the wonders Thomas was performing, could also see the wonders of the whole world. The icon at the west end of the reconstructed shrine makes reference to this plausible theory. *Reconstruction by Dan Terkla*

Receipt of London goldsmith John de Werleyngworth for £10 paid to him for his work on the shrine of St Thomas de Cantilupe in 1320. *Hereford Cathedral Archives 1440*

COMMEMORATING CANTILUPE

A S THOMAS'S FAME grew, he was commemorated not only in the cathedral where his relics were buried but also throughout the diocese of which he was bishop.

Thomas's personal heraldic crest followed that of his father, William II de Cantilupe. It features a red background with three fleurs-de-lys, with leopards' heads turned upside down, with the fleurs-de-lys issuing from their mouths (known as *jessant-de-lys*). Thomas's coat of arms became well known in Hereford Cathedral and parish churches where it was depicted carved in stone, in stained glass and in medieval wall painting. Bishop Adam Orleton utilised Thomas's arms on his own episcopal seal, featuring two of them, and it is after this time that the Cantilupe arms came to be regarded as the arms of the bishop and diocese of Hereford

The antiphon *Lux fulget in Anglia* (Salisbury Cathedral Library, MSS 224) reminds us of the close links between Cantilupe and other bishop-saints – in this case, St Osmond of Salisbury

Much of the liturgy for the feasts of St Thomas has resonances with existing material set for the feasts of St Thomas of Canterbury. Here we see a section of Second Vespers for the Feast of St Thomas – *Thomas primus fit doctor* – in a manuscript preserved in the Gloucestershire Archives (GDRZI/I4, fourteenth-century), perhaps from St Peter's Abbey

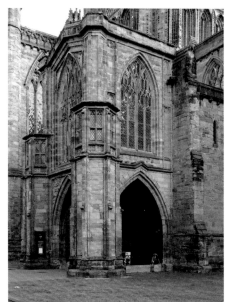

Above: Before the Booth Porch was installed, there was already a fourteenth-century north porch in place for pilgrims. This was completed during Bishop Richard's episcopate, and alludes to Hereford's place as a pilgrim destination, with many figures. One of the most prominent and visible as one enters the medieval porch, is this medieval pilgrim wearing his scrip and holding a staff

Right: Pilgrims to the shrine declined at the end of the fourteenth century; however, at times, efforts were made to revive interest in the saint. Bishop Richard Mayhew (1504–16) began a large north porch; work completed by his successor, Charles Booth (bishop 1516–35). The porch has two storeys, the uppermost forming a chapel with altars or shrines to the Blessed Virgin Mary and Our Lord. The porch is flanked by twin staircase turrets, one for ascent to the chapel, one for descent. These shrines may have provided part of the 'pilgrim experience' for those visiting the cathedral, with pilgrims proceeding from their devotions here, past the bishops' tombs to St Thomas's shrine in the Lady Chapel

The central tower of Hereford Cathedral, said to have been built with the support of large amounts of money left by pilgrims at the shrine of St Thomas. During the period Michaelmas 1290 to Michaelmas 1291, the total receipts amounted to £286.1s.8½d. Of this £178.10s.7d came from the tomb of the 'Blessed Thomas'. The total number of pilgrims involved can be estimated when it is remembered that the average offering would have been less than a penny. If every pilgrim donated a penny at the shrine, it would be expected that as many as 42,720 individuals had visited Thomas's tomb in this year

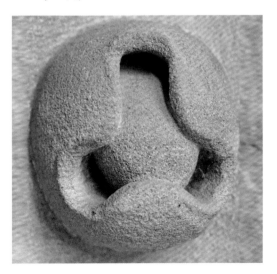

The distinctive ballflower carving, covering the central tower. The ballflower – a bud-like device with three petals enclosing a ball – is one of the defining motifs of Decorated Gothic architecture (c.1250–c.1350). The origins of the ballflower are uncertain. It appears in England and France in the twelfth century, and may ultimately derive from a horse- or hawk's bell, or possibly the globeflower (*trollius*)

The Audley Chapel, built to commemorate Edmund Audley, bishop of Hereford (1492–1502). The bishop was never buried here, as he was translated to Salisbury and is buried there in a similar chantry chapel, even including the detail of a boss with the Virgin in glory. The gallery above the chapel may have been a singing gallery or a 'Watching Chamber' from where watch could be kept on the shrine of St Thomas in the Lady Chapel below

The 'retrospective' series of bishops' tombs in the north and south choir aisles, dates from the fourteenth century. It seems to have formed part of a pilgrimage route around the cathedral, where pilgrims would first visit Thomas's tomb-shrine in the north transept, walk up the north choir aisle past five of the effigies, to the Lady Chapel, and then down the south choir aisle with another five effigies, to the south transept which may have held the Limoges reliquary casket containing a relic of Thomas Becket

Top left: Antiquarian drawings help us reconstruct the imagery around Thomas's tomb-shrine in the north transept. In one image by Thomas Dingley (d. 1695), there was a figure of St Thomas Becket, wearing vestments displaying Lombardic initial 'T's. This image shows a sketch by William Stukeley (1687–1765) of another painting showing Thomas de Cantilupe as bishop, wearing vestments with his heraldic arms of leopards' heads *jessant-de-lys*. *Oxford, Bodleian Library, MS Gen, Top. D.13, fol. 17*

Top right: St Thomas de Cantilupe with his wolf ('lupus'), St John the Baptist, Our Lady holding the Christ child, St Ethelbert the King, and St Thomas Becket. In the foreground are two angels, holding the Hereford Mappa Mundi. *The saints of Hereford, seen in the icon by Peter Murphy on the west end of the restored shrine*

Left: Many Hereford clergy were commemorated by monumental brasses. Among those which have survived is one to Richard Rudhale, archdeacon of Hereford (1546–76). He studied at Oxford and Padua, and wrote in law books which can be seen in the cathedral library. His monumental brass contains small figures of St Thomas of Hereford, St Ethelbert and St Thomas of Canterbury among others

One of the four main lights of the east window in the parish church of St Mary, Ross-on-Wye, dating to 1430. It was commissioned by Thomas Spofford, bishop of Hereford, for his episcopal palace at Stretton Sugwas, on the banks of the River Wye. This palace seems to have also been one of St Thomas's favourites, appearing often in the itinerary we can construct from his surviving episcopal register. The palace and chapel at Stretton Sugwas was pulled down in 1792, but its glass was described by antiquaries, and several of the main panes were sold and are now in the Church of St Mary the Virgin in Ross-on-Wye. Continuing associations with St Thomas of Canterbury, it is said that a window displaying him was near to that of St Thomas of Hereford in the chapel

Stained glass from Eaton Bishop, Herefordshire. The glass dates from the fourteenth century and is likely to have been installed not long after Thomas de Cantilupe was canonised. An inscription in one of the window panes notes that the principal donor was Adam Murimuth (d. 1347), a prominent fourteenth-century chronicler. Murimuth was a canon of Hereford Cathedral from 1 April 1320 to 12 February 1321. It is possible that the bishop depicted here is St Thomas of Hereford

Relics of St Thomas of Hereford

D URING THE LATE 1530s, the shrines of the saints were systematically dismantled and destroyed. By this time, the relics of the saint were in the Lady Chapel (placed there in 1349) and it was this shrine which was destroyed – possibly as late as 1548.

Before the commissioners arrived, it seems that the relics were removed from the shrine and were held in honour by the recusant Catholic community. In 1609/10 the relics were carried in procession at night to ask the saint's intercession in averting the plague. It has been estimated that perhaps a fifth of Hereford's population in the seventeenth century retained their attachment to the old religion and their veneration for St Thomas de Cantilupe was very strong.

Several of St Thomas's relics found their way to the Jesuit college of St Omer and to a community in north Wales, associated with the shrine at Holywell. At the latter, the tibia was cared for and, in 1835, transferred to Stonyhurst, where it was provided with a reliquary made by Hardman of Birmingham. The reliquary's two ends are ornamented in silver with the armorial bearings of the Cantilupes

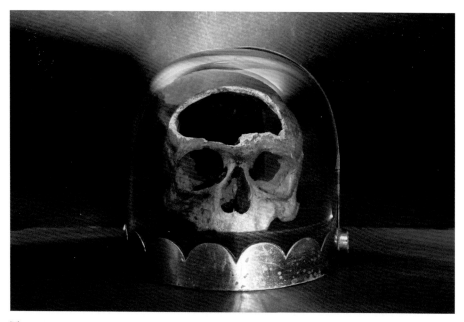

Thomas's skull is said to have been kept in a house in Hereford, until a lay brother of the Benedictine community of Lamspring in Germany, when visiting the house in 1670, discovered the skull and took it to his monastery, where it remained until 1881. It was rediscovered and brought back to the Benedictine community at Downside, where it remains today, placed in an ark designed by Sir Ninian Comper. The skull has a piece removed from its front and, like the relic at Stonyhurst, has the unmistakeable colouring caused by the boiling after the saint's death

Left: The relic in Belmont Abbey, given to the community in 1959, is thought to be a section removed from St Thomas's skull. *Right*: Relic of St Thomas preserved in the Medici Chapels, Florence

THE SHRINE AFTER THE REFORMATION

THE EARLIEST DESCRIPTION we have of the shrine post-Reformation is in Francis Godwin's *Catalogue of the Bishops of England, since the first planting of Christian religion in this Island*. A later historian, Thomas Dingley, in his *History from Marble*, gives a description of the tomb, 'whence his body was translated to this city and interr'd under this famous high tomb'.

The rise of tourism in the eighteenth century, and of the Wye Valley tour, saw Hereford visited more, with new guide books emphasising the curiosity of the surviving shrine. Thus, Samuel Ireland, writing in 1797, noted: 'Some monuments of their bishops still remain, among which, in the north wing, is the Shrine of Bishop Cantilupe. The monument of the family of the Bohuns, in the library is *curious*, [author's italics] and deserved the attention of the antiquary.'

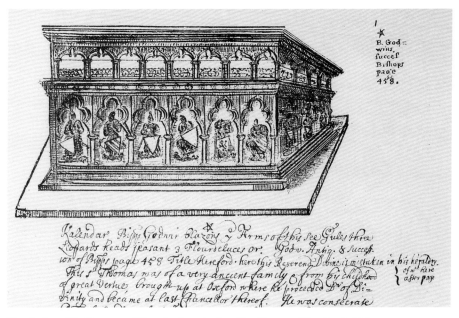

The shrine of St Thomas of Hereford, as depicted by Thomas Dingley (*1684*)

48

Cantilupe Remembered and Revived

THE NINETEENTH CENTURY saw a revival in interest in the saints. For Roman Catholics this meant an increased focus on the relics of saints, both pre- and post-Reformation. For Anglicans this meant a celebration of the saints, not as reasons for ritual devotion but as examples of faith and courage. With the rediscovery of the ministry of cathedrals, saints achieved a new prominence, and, as their buildings were restored by the Victorians, so images of the saints proliferated – in glass, stone and wood. The feasts of saints were again celebrated and major anniversaries of dioceses linked to the lives of patron saints. Hereford was no exception and, from the middle of the nineteenth century, interest in St Thomas revived.

Top left: St Thomas of Hereford appears embroidered on the frontal completed in 1876 to commemorate the 1,200th anniversary of the foundation of the diocese in 676

Bottom left: The inner porch was completed in 1925, as a memorial to Dean James Leigh. It has a statue of St Thomas in full pontifical vestments

Left: The stained glass window in the south transept is by the firm of C.E. Kempe. It dates from 1895 and is Kempe's largest single window. It commemorates George Herbert, dean 1868–93, and represents a text from *Te Deum Laudamus*: 'the glorious company of the apostles praise thee'. Pevsner called it 'pedestrian and parochial', but it is particularly interesting in its depiction of local saints – St Thomas of Hereford, St Dubricius and St Ethelbert

Top left: A key development occurred in the late 1970s, when there was a scheme to interpret the shrine for a contemporary generation. What emerged was the 'Nimbus', a metal creation by David Watkins, which was dedicated in 1981. David Watkins describes the Nimbus thus: 'The shape and position of the tomb suggested a horizontal, overhead object, which in turn suggested the symbolism of floating in space, and defying gravity. The object was visualised as a marker in space and position of the saint, to be seen from a distance, but understood only from close quarters [...] In my mind, the overall form is a metaphor of a sound – a chord or mantra – suggesting calm and repose.'

Top right: In 1982, the 700th anniversary of the death of St Thomas, the diocese received a visit from Dr Robert Runcie, 102nd archbishop of Canterbury (1980–91). Here he is shown kneeling at the shrine with John Eastaugh, the 102nd bishop of Hereford (1974–90)

Bottom left: During 1982, Bishop John Eastaugh made a pilgrimage around many of the churches in the diocese

Bottom right: During the same festival year, the cathedral was visited by HRH The Princess Margaret, who is pictured here at the shrine

Left: By the 1990s, the shrine base itself was showing signs of deterioration, and a major archaeological survey and reconstruction was undertaken. The shrine base was dismantled, studied and reassembled, with opportunities taken for scholarly reassessment of this extraordinary survival. It is a topic still explored today, with an article by Sally Badham for the *Transactions of the Monumental Brass Society* convincingly laying out the chronology of the shrine's construction. It is thought that the monumental brass, one of the first in the country, had been laid when Thomas was interred in the Lady Chapel. It was then moved, on its stone, and trimmed to size to fit an altar-tomb. Sometime later a feretory was added with apertures for pilgrims to place afflicted limbs into, to get as close to the saint as possible

Bottom: Donors to the refurbishment scheme included the Friends of Hereford Cathedral, who are seen here at the dedication of the new shrine altar

Salve Thoma pastor bone

dies at Oxford and Paris   Thomas becomes Chancellor of
England

ministers to his   Thomas disputes with Archbishop
Pecham and is excommunicated

Cantilupe Today

Today St Thomas of Hereford is honoured each year in his cathedral. His feast, on 2 October, is observed with a Eucharist, Evensong and Procession to the shrine. The College of Canons also meets on 2 October, or thereabouts, and there is an annual 'Cantilupe Lecture' to celebrate St Thomas, bringing in noted medieval historians to talk about an aspect of St Thomas's life, death and miracles.

The shrine serves as a focus for prayer and intercession, and each day many pilgrims leave their prayers and light a candle. Prayers are often used in public worship and are clearly a very important part of our ministry of prayer and hospitality to our visitors and pilgrims.

Between 2002 and 2005, the Friends of Hereford Cathedral made a pilgrimage, following in the footsteps of St Thomas and adhering to the route of his final journey in 1282. In four sections, the journey covered 1,200 miles and ended at La Badia, near Orvieto. There, at the possible site of the burial of St Thomas's flesh in August 1282, Michael Tavinor, dean of Hereford, and June Chase, secretary of the Friends, laid roses in remembrance of the saint

Opposite: The shrine base stood in the north transept of the cathedral, a beautiful example of medieval craftsmanship; however, with the development of pilgrimage in the cathedral, something more engaging and attractive was clearly needed. The shrine refurbishment was carried out under the direction of cathedral architect, Robert Kilgour, supported by craftsmen Stephen Florence, Peter Murphy and Neil Lossock. The newly-refurbished shrine was brought into use on 8 November 2008 and dedicated by the bishop of Hereford, the Right Revd Anthony Priddis. A relic of St Thomas was handed over to the bishop by the abbots of Downside and Belmont – symbolising the new-found unity which the shrine expresses

Above left: In 2009–11, the Cathedral Close was refurbished, and bronze medallions were inserted at ground level, depicting key scenes from the cathedral's history. One shows an interpretation of elements of the shine with its arches and knights

Above right: The scallop shell is a traditional symbol of pilgrimage, from its association with the journey to Santiago de Compostela. Here it provides a threshold marker, welcoming pilgrims who arrive through the pilgrim entrance to the cathedral, the Booth Porch

St Thomas was baptised in Hambleden Church in 1218, and on the 800th anniversary year, the choir and congregation visited Hereford Cathedral and were presented with pilgrim badges. The Friends of Hereford Cathedral visited Hambleden Church in August 2018 and renewed their Baptismal vows at the font where Cantilupe was baptised. Pictured above are the Dean, Michael Tavinor, and the Canon Chancellor, Christopher Pullin

Near the shrine, pilgrims and visitors light candles and leave intercessions, to be used in regular worship at the cathedral. St Thomas's shrine continues its original purpose as a focus for prayer and healing

Above left: Designed by Alison Merry for the start of the 2019–20 celebrations of the 700th anniversary of St Thomas's canonisation, these Christmas cards show images of pilgrims arriving at the shrine – young and old, lay and religious, rich and poor. The arches of the design take their inspiration from St Thomas's shrine, as does the brilliant colouring

Above right: Pilgrim badges, usually made of lead alloy, were often obtained at pilgrim sites as souvenirs. Most popular were pilgrim badges from Canterbury, which have a great variety of imagery, including badges of St Thomas Becket's shrine, his head and scenes from his life. St Thomas de Cantilupe's badge, designed by Sandy Elliott for the 2020 celebrations, shows him in bishop's vestments, with his family shield and his faithful wolf by his side

Above: Activities during the St Thomas Way inauguration day in 2018. Pilgrims are 'measured' to the saint, with a wick held against each person to measure their height. The wick is then covered in wax, and the resulting candle placed near the shrine. This was a medieval devotional practice noted in St Thomas's miracle collection, and appears to have its origins in the story of Elijah stretching himself over the body of a Zarephathite woman's son (*1 Kings 17, verse 21*)

Right: Pilgrims pray for healing at the shrine

A new banner, made for the 2020 celebrations and taking its inspiration from the window in Credenhill church, depicting England's two Thomases: Cantilupe and Becket, together. The banner was designed by Sandy Elliott and made by the Cathedral Broderers, under the direction of Margaret Gardner. It was dedicated by Bishop Richard Frith in October 2019

Top: St Thomas Cantilupe School. In buildings of the early twentieth century, the school was renamed in 1984 and opened by the then bishop, John Eastaugh

Bottom: Pupils of St Thomas Cantilupe School and Hereford Cathedral Junior School re-enact the saint's story, in the opening service of the 700th anniversary celebrations for Cantilupe's canonisation. The preacher was Baron Williams of Oystermouth, 104th archbishop of Canterbury (2003–12), who is shown here speaking to the children

Prayers and Texts in Honour of St Thomas of Hereford

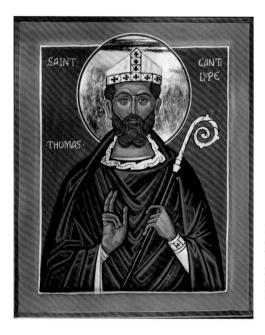

Icon of St Thomas
of Hereford, written
by Sandy Elliott as
part of a week-long
master class, led by
Peter Murphy

Collect

Almighty God, glorified in all your saints, who gave grace to your
servant Thomas of Hereford steadfastly to resist evil and uphold
justice: grant that we who commemorate his holy life and angelic
virtues may likewise live blamelessly and rebuke vice, that we may
win with him an eternal crown; through our Lord and Saviour Jesus
Christ who is alive and reigns with you and the Holy Spirit, one God,
now and for ever. *Amen*

Hymn

God, Creator, wise and loving,
God mysterious, past all proving,
Father of all souls that be;
May we share in love and giving
With Saint Thomas hope of living
In one caring family.

Christ, who lost your life to save us,
Through the cross new vision gave us
Christ, unfailing friend today;
Pilgrims may we, form or failing,
With our saint proclaim your calling
You, the Life, the Truth, the Way.

Holy Spirit, thoughts unfolding,
Treasures hope for our beholding
On our endless pilgrimage;
As we think and strive and ponder,
May we live in daily wonder
At your presence, age by age.

Trinity, whose love has brought us
Pilgrims here, where Thomas taught us,
Humble healer, bishop, sage;
All with him your faith confessing,
Send us with your daily blessing
On our Christian pilgrimage.

H.C.A. Gaunt 1902–83

Responsory for the feast day – 2 October

Thomas primus fit doctor gencium,
Alter ensis subit supplicium:
Hic pastoris complet officium,
Binum prebens se sacrificium.
Carne licet non sensit gladium,
Corde tamen suplet martirium.

The first Thomas [the Apostle] *became
a teacher of the people*

The other [Thomas Becket] *underwent
the punishment of the sword:*

This one [Thomas de Cantilupe]
completed the office of shepherd,

*Providing himself as a double sacrifice.
Although he did not suffer the sword
bodily,*

He achieved martyrdom in his heart.

Antiphon for Vespers throughout the octave of St Thomas's feast

Salve Thoma pastor bone,
Christi gregis et patrone,
Ac doctor ecclesie;
Opem queso fer ergotis.
Atque mentibus devotis,
confer lumen gracis.

*Hail, Thomas! Good pastor,
the flock of Christ, and patron,
and doctor of the Church;
Bring to the sick the power of our petitions,
And on devout minds,
Bestow the light of grace.*

Wall-painting in Barton Church, Cambridgeshire, dating from c.1350. It depicts a bishop wearing vestments, with the Cantilupe arms of leopards' heads *jessant-de-lys*. At his feet is a small figure in prayer. The painting was uncovered in 1929 and is the only known surviving wall-painting of St Thomas of Hereford

St Thomas de Cantilupe
Hereford Cathedral's Third Patron Saint [1]

by Ian Bass

O N 20 September 1320, five months after the canonisation of St Thomas de Cantilupe, bishop of Hereford (1275–82), Bishop Adam Orleton of Hereford (1317–27) wrote a letter which called on all the faithful to celebrate St Thomas's first official feast day of 2 October.[2] Towards the end of the letter, Bishop Adam stated: 'For we, through the mercy of Almighty God, are confident in the meritorious intercessions of His glorious mother, the Virgin Mary, the Blessed Ethelbert the king and martyr, and Saint Thomas, bishop and confessor, our patrons.'[3] Thus, almost four centuries after the appropriation of its second patron saint, the bishop of Hereford seemingly appointed Hereford Cathedral's third, and it was thereafter the Cathedral of Saint Mary the Virgin, Saint Ethelbert the king and martyr, and Saint Thomas the bishop and confessor. Even though this final patronal association is not made today, St Thomas de Cantilupe's medieval cult had an undeniable impact on the fabric of Hereford Cathedral – an impact modern visitors come from far and wide to admire.[4]

The purpose of this essay is to celebrate the 700th anniversary of St Thomas of Hereford's canonisation and to provide a general overview of some of the miracles performed by Hereford's third patron saint. The essay is thus divided into three sections. The first gives an overview of the available miracle collection. The second places St Thomas alongside his co-patrons of Hereford Cathedral by exploring two miracles where he explicitly appears alongside Mary and Ethelbert, as well as examining other saintly associations evident in the collection and in iconography. Finally, the essay provides a short examination of the entirety of St Thomas's cult and the number of cures contained in the miracle collection.

ST THOMAS AND HIS MIRACLES

On Maundy Thursday, 3 April 1287, a large crowd gathered in Hereford Cathedral for the celebrations of Holy Week and Easter. At some point during the day, Richard de Swinfield, bishop of Hereford (1283–1317), and the dean and chapter of the cathedral solemnly translated the bones of Thomas de Cantilupe from where they had originally rested in the Lady Chapel, to a new, bespoke tomb in the north transept. At the new tomb a mass for the dead was celebrated. Soon after, word spread that someone had received a miracle. John de Massington, one of Bishop Richard's foresters on his Bosbury estate, had been afflicted with blindness for two years, but after praying at the new tomb and invoking Bishop Thomas's name, he received his sight.[5] By the end of the day five more cures from blindness had been witnessed and a miraculous cult was soon in full swing.

This was the first officially recorded miracle performed by Thomas de Cantilupe. The miracles attested at Bishop Thomas's tomb from 1287 onwards were thereafter recorded in lists by custodians present at the shrine, and were added to continuously until 1312.[6] A later fourteenth-century account by the chronicler John of Tynemouth, gives the indication that there might have been many more volumes of miracles, stating that records were kept 'at his [Thomas's] resting place in such diverse volumes that they seemed as if infinite.'[7]

The surviving manuscript known as Oxford, Exeter College, MS 158 forms the chronological list of miracles reported at Bishop Thomas's tomb from 1287 to 1312.[8] The manuscript comprises two sections. Folios 1r to 47v comprise the records of 432 miraculous cures reported to and recorded by the custodians at the tomb in the north transept. Folios 48r to 59v contain a copy of a report written from 1318 to 1320 by a member of the papal court on Thomas's life and miracles, with a critical study of 26 miracles examined by witness testimony, providing objections and replies in order to prove whether they were bona fide cures. It was this report, with the agreement of the cardinals, that gave Pope John XXII (1316–34) enough evidence to canonise Thomas de Cantilupe on 17 April 1320.[9] One final miracle is written in the collection, on folio 60r, and dates to 1404.

The other material of paramount importance to the study of St Thomas's life, death and miracles, is the documentary evidence derived from the canonisation inquiry held in Hereford and London between July and November 1307 (Vatican, Biblioteca Apostolica Vaticana, Vat. Cod. Lat. 4015).[10] It comprises 314 folios and is in three sections. The first, folios 1r–122v, provide accounts of the witness testimony given on Thomas's life, death and some miracles. The second, folios 123r–264r, record further testimony on miracles, as well as other papal and episcopal letters about Thomas's pluralism, and letters from bishops and others requesting his canonisation. Finally, folios 265r–316v contain a copy of the miracles in Exeter 158, as well as a final report by one of the papal commissioners.

In total the records here provide accounts of 461 miraculous cures reported for the period 1287 to 1404 – the second highest tally of miracles by an English saint after St Thomas Becket, archbishop of Canterbury (1162–70, canonised 1173). VL 4015 has also been recognised as a document of paramount interest to scholars of medieval Church history, as it contains the largest extant record of a medieval canonisation.[11] It is from these records that many studies have been conducted in recent years, the most notable of which is Robert Bartlett's *The Hanged Man* (2004) which focuses on the death and resuscitation of the Welsh brigand, William Cragh. The research of this book has resulted in a documentary, and has been utilised as part of the public-facing projects of Swansea City Witness and the modern pilgrimage route from Swansea to Hereford, the St Thomas Way.[12]

It might well be that the posthumous miracle-performing powers exhibited by Bishop Thomas's bones on this day and afterwards had been anticipated by the Hereford chapter and bishop. In 1286 Bishop Richard wrote to his proctors in Italy to investigate whether a holy spring associated with Thomas – outside the monastery of San Severo (Orvieto) at the site where Bishop Thomas's body had been boiled – had performed any miracles.[13] Moreover, on Palm Sunday, 30 March 1287, Bishop Thomas was reported to have performed his first miracle. Edith, the wife of Robert the ironmonger of Hereford, was cured of her madness as a consequence of a vision of the bishop.[14] It was reported that Edith attacked her mother and husband, and blasphemed against God. She was brought to Hereford Cathedral and spent time bound before the altar of the Holy Cross in the rood loft and at the altar of the Virgin Mary in the Lady Chapel for a week. Edith's husband reported that while she spent the day in prayer before the altar of the Virgin, near the place where Bishop Thomas's bones were stored ahead of their translation, she suddenly had a vision of the bishop and was cured.[15] Others reported that during a Palm Sunday mass occurring at the same time, all the candles in the building were simultaneously extinguished, with no indication of any wind to explain the eerie event.[16] This celebration at the cathedral was soon put down by Thomas of St Omer, the official of Bishop Thomas's nemesis, Archbishop John Peckham of Canterbury (1279–92), and the miracle was instead attributed to Bishop John le Breton of Hereford (1269–75).[17] Nevertheless, the cult of St Thomas of Hereford took off, with miracles being performed from 3 April 1287 onwards, generating pilgrimage to Hereford from much of England, Wales and Ireland.

ST THOMAS AMONG THE SAINTS

In view of St Thomas of Hereford's placement as the third patron saint in the pantheon of Hereford Cathedral, and in the light of the miracle collections in Exeter 158 and VL 4015, it is worth dwelling here on St Thomas's interactions with other saints, particularly the two other patrons, the Virgin Mary and St Ethelbert. In Exeter 158 and VL 4015 there are two miracles which explicitly record interactions between St Thomas and the other patrons. It has been seen fit to quote the entries in their entirety here together with full transcriptions and translations. The Latin is taken from Exeter 158, with notes on variations in spelling in VL 4015 noted below.

The first account is dated to 8 February 1292 and contains the report of a vision of St Thomas appearing alongside St Ethelbert to Robert the leatherworker from Staffordshire after he had been left for dead by robbers.

> *Item . vj . idus Februarii vir quidam nomine Robertus le Cutiller de Chatculne' in Comitatu Stafford' Conventr' et Lichef' diocesis asseruit ad tumulum viri dei quod cum se sicut mos est mercatoribus causa lucre ad loca diuersa transferret incidit in latrones qui spoliauerunt eum et multis plagis mortiferis in positis abierunt ipso[a] non solum semiuiuo sed[b] quasi mortuo derelicto. Et sic iacuit quasi mortuus*

67

et a Cirugicis et medicis desperatus per diem integrum nat-
uralem. Et tunc quidam amicorum ipsius ipsum viro dei
vouerunt. Et mox sibi apparuerunt ut postmodum retulit
dum sic iaceret quasi in extasi rex unus et unus pontifex
stantes etiam^c iuxta eum. Et ipse Episcopus sic ei apercis-
sime loquebatur. Ecce recuperabis protinus sanitatem, et
postea ecclesiam istius Regis Ethelberti peregre visitabis.
Et hiis dictis ambo disperverunt Rex videlicet et pontifex
memoratus. Et ipse recepit integram sanitatem per merita
viri dei.

(a) ipso] ipsum **V**; (b) sed] set **V**; (c) etiam] omitted in **V**.

Likewise, on the sixth ides of February [8 February 1292], a man called Robert le Cutiller [the leather-worker], who was from Chatcull[?] in the county of Staffordshire and the diocese of Coventry and Lichfield, asserted at the tomb of the man of God that when, as is the custom for merchants, he was travelling to diverse places for the sake of profit, he got caught up with thieves. These robbed him and fled, leaving him not so much half-alive as basically dead from the dispensation of many fatal injuries. And so he lay as if dead for the whole of one day, despaired of by surgeons and doctors. And then some of his friends offered him to the man of God. And afterwards, as he later recounted, a king and a bishop appeared to him while he lay as if in a trance, even standing next to him. And the bishop spoke to him most frankly with these words: "You will recover your full health and afterwards you must visit the church of this king, Ethelbert, on pilgrimage." And when this had been said, they both vanished – the king and the bishop just mentioned, that is. And he received full health through the merits of the man of God.[18]

In a way, this is a curious miracle, as Thomas advises the man only to come to the cathedral at Hereford and not to his own tomb as he does at other times. St Ethelbert, furthermore, seems to appear only in a supporting role, lending his weight to the veracity of Thomas's words and silently standing by his side during the vision. On the other hand, it is the first miracle to demonstrate that Thomas had been accepted as a patron of Hereford Cathedral, standing side by side with Ethelbert proffering his silent endorsement of this new cult.

An implicit association with Ethelbert was, however, made in an earlier miracle reported originally in 1288. It is an important account, especially since it was examined in the 1307 canonisation inquiry and was found to be a bona fide cure, and thus included in the papal bull of canonisation in 1320.[19] On 21 April 1288, Johanna le Schirreve and her father appeared at the tomb, having travelled from Marden. It was reported that Johanna had drowned and been resuscitated by the merits of Thomas de Cantilupe.[20] Nineteen years later, during the canonisation inquiry, the events of the story were elaborated.[21] At the event of her resuscitation, she had been measured to Thomas

> and when that girl had revived somewhat, the men carried her to the parish church of the aforementioned place around daybreak and placed her at the altar of Saint Ethelbert the king and martyr, patron of the church of Hereford.[22]

In some ways this was a double dedication to both saintly intercessors at Hereford Cathedral, even though later witness testimony wholly attributed the cure to Thomas's powers. In fact, Johanna herself emphasised that she became somewhat of a local celebrity, having not taken a husband, and was proclaimed in the parish as the 'virgin of St Thomas'.[23] The significance of Marden itself as the location of the cure cannot be understated, since the church was founded at the site where a miraculous spring associated with St Ethelbert had welled up after his murder.[24] While the association of the two saints in this account may have been more implicit, the fact that while Thomas was invoked she was taken to the parish church of St Ethelbert would not have been lost on the cathedral authorities.

The second account dates to Whit-Sunday, 6 June 1294, when the Virgin Mary and Thomas appear in a vision to William Talgar. William was imprisoned for some misdemeanour against his territorial lord, for which he was later found innocent.

Item anno eodem . viij . idus Iunii vir quidam Willelmus Talgar nomine cum per dominum suum terrenum innocens fuisset missus in Carcerem et tanto pondere ferri[a] constrictus ut eius sinistrum brachium frangeretur. Cum ipse tam squalore carceris quam fractura predicta nimium torqueretur pro sua liberacione et sanitate servi dei auxilium invocavit votum emittens quod eius tumulum in persona propria visitaret quamcito ipsum contingeret a carcere liberati. Et ecce brachio eius statim sanato et ipso in brevi postmodum de carceralibus vinculis liberato: Ille sui Benefactoris et voti factus immemor et ingratus processu temporis gravissime egrotabat in tantum: ut frenesim incurrerat et fieret velut[b] arrepticius a demonibus cruciatus ut sibi videbatur in sompnis. Et in tantum torquebatur insanus: ut brachium eius frangeretur in loco ubi primitus fuit fractum. Et cum quadam vice aliquantulum dormitaret vidit in sompnis gloriosissimam matrem dei dicentem servo dei Thome[c] pontifici qui ut sibi videbatur tunc astabat ibidem. Amice adiuua miserum istum. *Qui statim respondit Virgini gloriose.* Illusit mihi[d] homo iste

promisit enim quod me ante hec tempora visitasset et
non venit ut redderet votum suum. *Et mater misericordie
iterum dixit ei.* Ipse veniet ad te adiuua illum rogo. *At
ille respondit.* Veniat tunc de Pentecost' et sanabitur in
nomine domini. *Quibus dictis venerabilis virgo disparvit
et vir dei similiter. Ipse autem vir predictus referens astan-
tibus visionem postmodum ductus est ad tumulum viri dei,
die predicta scilicet que fuit . viij . idus Iunii. Et ibidem tam
et brachii⁰ fraccione quam a frenetica passione ipsa die fuit
divinitus liberatus per intercessionem virginis gloriose et
merita servi dei predicti.*

(a) ferri] fieri V; (b) velut] velud V; (c) servo dei Thome] servo
Thome dei V; (d) mihi] michi V; (e) et brachii] abrachii V.

Likewise, in the same year [1294], on the eighth ides
of June [6 June]: when a man called William Talgar,
although innocent, was sent to jail by his terrestrial lord,
the iron that bound him was so heavy that his left arm
was broken. While he was being excessively tortured as
much by the squalor of the jail as by the fracture, he
called upon the aid of the servant of God for his free-
dom and health, vowing that he would visit his tomb
in person if it transpired that he was freed from the
jail. But when his arm was immediately healed and he
was freed from the chains that imprisoned him, a short
while later he forgot his benefactor and his vow. With
the passing of time, that ungrateful individual became
very gravely sickened to such an extent that madness
took hold of him and made it seem as if he were seized
and tortured by demons that appeared to him in his
sleep. And that insane individual was tortured so much
that his arm was broken in the same place where it had
been before. And when on one occasion he was sleeping,
he saw in his sleep the most glorious Mother of God

speaking to Bishop Thomas, the servant of God, who, as it seemed to him, was standing there: "Friend, help this miserable individual." He responded at once to the glorious Virgin: "The man mocked me. For he promised before now that he would visit me and he did not come to redeem his vow." And the Mother of Mercy spoke to him again: "He will come to you, I ask you to help him." And he responded: "Then let him come for Pentecost [6 June] and he will be healed in the Lord's name." When these things had been said, the venerable Virgin disappeared and the man of God also. That man, however, recounting his vision to those standing by was afterwards led to the tomb of the man of God on the day mentioned above, namely the eighth ides of June [6 June]. And he was divinely freed there on that day not only from the fracture, but from the madness which he suffered, through the intercession of the glorious Virgin and the merits of the aforementioned servant of God.[25]

The appearance of the Virgin Mary in this account is incredibly important for demonstrating Thomas de Cantilupe's acceptance in the pantheon of Hereford's saints, especially because she is the principal patron of the cathedral. Thomas's attitude in the miracle is somewhat remarkable. Instead of simply complying with the Virgin and healing the man a second time (especially after she tells Thomas to help him) Thomas remains stubborn and indicates that he will only heal the man when he comes to Hereford Cathedral. In many ways, it seems to conform to the steadfast personality that we can construct from the historical record. It is also possible that we might view this as a dual miracle again, much like Johanna le Schirreve's above, with Mary interceding with Thomas to heal the man a second time, since if the Virgin did not support Thomas as a miracle-performing saint she could have easily cured the man herself.[26] In fulfilling the vow, the man ventured to the cathedral where Mary was the principal saintly patron, and then to the shrine of his healer.

It is possible that a third account in the miracle collection brings all three patron saints together. The entry concerns Walter Boton, a cleric of Corfe Castle in Dorset, who was suffering from a severe illness in 1291. When his friends exhausted all medical options, he appears to have been visited in visions by a woman and a young man associated in some way with Thomas.

> *Item . xv . kalendas Septembris aderant ad viri dei tumu-*
> *lum referentes quod quidam clericus nomine Walterus dictus*
> *Boton de Corf castell' in Comitatu de Dorsete, Sarr' dioce-*
> *sis, tam graviter fuerat infirmatus quod ab omnibus amicis*
> *et medicis credebatur protinus moriturus. Cum igitur nullo*
> *posset vivari auxilio medicorum sed quasi mortuus credere-*
> *tur amici ipsius presentes ipsum viro dei cum devocione*
> *magna voverunt. Et ecce statim ipsis cernentibus apperebat*
> *more viventium se movere, et ipsi infirmo ut postmodum*
> *retulit videbatur quod quidam puer elegantis forme ad se*
> *attulit quandam cortinam quam per lecti sui circuitum*
> *decenter composuit et suspendit, quem puerum sequebatur*
> *quedam Femina splendidissime venustatis capud cuiusdam*
> *episcopi portans in manibus reverenter. Hec dicens infirmo.*
> Ecce capud beati Thome de Cantilupo per quod recip-
> ies sanitatem. *Et hiis dictis: confestim euanuit. Et ecce*
> *protinus supervenit quidam iuvenis aspectu pulcherrimus*
> *ducens Episcopum unum secum sacerdotalibus vestimentis*
> *indutum dicens infirmo.* Huic Episcopo gratias age cuius
> auxilio recipies sanitatem. *Et cum hec[a] dixisset statim*
> *disperuiter. Et ipse infirmus protinus se invenit ab omnibus*
> *angustiis liberatum et sanum per merita viri dei.*

(a) hec] hoc **V**.

73

Likewise, on the fifteenth kalends of September [18 August], some people came to the tomb of the man of God who reported that a cleric called Walter Boton, who was from Corfe Castle in the county of Dorset and the diocese of Salisbury, had been so greatly weakened by illness that all of his friends and doctors believed that he was about to die. Therefore, when he could not be saved by the doctors' aid but was believed to be more or less dead, his friends offered him to the man of God with great devotion. And at once they perceived that he appeared to move himself in the manner of the living. And the sick man recounted afterwards that it seemed as if a boy of elegant form produced a drape from himself which he properly arranged and suspended around his bed. A very splendid woman followed the boy, carrying the beautiful head of that bishop reverently in her hands. She spoke to the sick man: "see the head of the Blessed Thomas de Cantilupe through which you will receive health." After she had said these things she immediately vanished. And then a young man came in who was very beautiful in appearance, leading a bishop clothed in priestly vestments with him and saying to the sick man: "give thanks to this bishop through the help of whom you will receive health." And when he had said this he suddenly disappeared. And the sick man discovered immediately afterwards that he was freed from all suffering and that he was well through the merits of the man of God.[27]

While the figures in the account are described in a vague manner, we must not forget that the information here is third hand. Walter the cleric told his friends of the vision that he had, and they, in turn, reported it to the registrars in Hereford at Thomas's tomb, who then decided to translate it into Latin and record it. It is plausible that, if

Walter himself had come to report the cure, he might have been able to elaborate more on the identity of the woman who appeared with Thomas's head and the man who appeared alongside the bishop. There is, however, a case to be made for the figures to represent the Virgin Mary and Ethelbert. First, the language describing the woman is similar to the hyperbolic language used in the other miracle account in which she appears, as well as to medieval descriptions of Mary in prayers and other devotional texts. Secondly, while the man is not described as a king, it is generally accepted that Ethelbert was a young man when he was murdered. Finally, we must consider that the two other miracles above are the only times when Thomas appears alongside other saints in the miracle collection. This miracle predates both, and we might be able to conclude that the cathedral authorities were cautious in their first description of Thomas standing alongside his fellow co-patrons until such a time as another, similar vision was reported.

We should also consider two other saints in association with St Thomas. The first relates to a miracle. On 20 April 1294 Walter of Chewton Mendip, from the diocese of Bath and Wells, reported his cure. He had suffered from blindness and, while in prayer at an altar of the Anglo-Saxon abbess, St Etheldreda of Ely (d. 679), he had a vision. St Etheldreda appeared to him and told him: "Go to the tomb of Saint Thomas who is at Hereford and there you will receive the health you desire."[28] Walter was taken to Hereford and thus received his sight. This is the first of only two times Thomas de Cantilupe is referred to as a saint in the miracle collection, and it seems to have been especially significant that a well-established Anglo-Saxon saint confirmed Thomas's place firmly among the pantheon of English saints.[29] Why St Etheldreda was the one to do this is curious, and an explanation for the association is yet to be found.

The final association we must consider is St Thomas de Cantilupe's placement as a second St Thomas Becket.[30] This saintly association is most prevalent in iconography, some of which can still be seen around Hereford Cathedral, as well as in texts for the feast of St Thomas of Hereford. The texts available, such as the responsory for 2 October in the thirteenth-century Hereford Breviary, clearly demonstrated the second St Thomas's placement among the other two: St Thomas the Apostle and St Thomas of Canterbury.[31] The association was far more explicit, however, in the imagery. From the late twelfth century, Hereford had possession of a Limoges reliquary chasse depicting Becket's martyrdom and containing a relic of the saint. It is likely that this reliquary formed part of the pilgrimage experience at Hereford.[32] From antiquarian images by Thomas Dingley and William Stukeley we know that painted images depicting the two Thomases were painted near each other: St Thomas of Canterbury holding a cross-staff and vestments emblazoned with Lombardic 'T's, and St Thomas of Hereford with a crozier and vestments with the Cantilupe arms of leopards' heads *jessant-de-lys*.[33] Furthermore, two windows and two funerary monuments around the cathedral had images of the two Thomases.[34]

ST THOMAS'S MIRACLES: A STATISTICAL OVERVIEW [35]

Finally, it is worth giving a short précis of the statistical composition of St Thomas of Hereford's cult and its participants.[36] As shown in Table One opposite, recent calculations based on the manuscript evidence show that Exeter 158 records a total of 431 miracles for the period 1287 to 1312, and VL 4015 contains 435 for 1287 to 1307. When we collate the miracles missing from Exeter 158 – omitted primarily as a result of the loss of some folios during the fifteenth-century rebinding – we find that a total of 461 miraculous cures was recorded.

Year 3 April – 2 April	Exeter 158 folios	No. of Miracles	VL 4015 folios	No. of Miracles
1287–88	1r–7r	166	267r–274r	156
1288–89	7r–10v	34	274r–277v	36
1289–90	10v–14v	27	277v–281v	27
1290–91	14v–19v	40	281v–287r	40
1291–92	19v–21v	18	287r–289r	19
1292–93	21v–24r	20	289r–291r	21
1293–94	24r–25v	11	291r–292v	11
1294–95	25v–28r	16	292v–295r	16
1295–96	28r–29r	3	295r–296r	8
1296–97	29r–33r	18	296r–301r	32
1297–98	33r–33v	0	301r	0
1298–99	33v	1	301r–302r	6
1299–1300	33v, 35r	8	302r–303r	10
1300–01	33v, 34v, 35r, 35v	9	303r–304r	9
1301–02	34v, 36r	8	304r–304v	8
1302–03	36r–38r	19	304v–307v	20
1303–04	38r–39v	8	307v–309v	8
1304–05	39v–40r	4	309v–310r	4
1305–06	40r–41r	5	310r–310v	4
1306–07	41r	0	310v	0
1307–08	41r	0	310v	0
1308–09	41r–v	2	—	—
1309–10	41v–43v	7	—	—
1310–11	44v–46r	3	—	—
1311–12	46r–47v	3	—	—
1312	47v	1	—	—
1404	60r	1	—	—
Total No. of Miracles		432		435

Table One: The numbers of miracles in Exeter 158 and VL 4015

In breaking down the miracle collection in this way, several interesting observations can be made regarding some irregularities in the figures, as well as some general conclusions about the overall cult. The irregularities seem to be concentrated in the years 1290 to 1291 and 1306 to 1308.

The first irregularity is an unusually large increase in the miraculous cures reported and recorded in the year April 1290 to April 1291, providing the second highest total in the collection. This boom seems to correlate directly with a pronounced period of promotion spurred by Bishop Richard de Swinfield. It is probable that an ecclesiastical council was held in London in early January 1290. At this meeting Bishop Richard petitioned his brother bishops to lend their support to the cult.[37] From an intensive examination of the miracle accounts, it can be seen that almost half of all 1290 to 1291's recorded miracle recipients came from the dioceses of bishops we can place in London at the same time. Likewise, an increase in pilgrimage seems to have been inspired by Bishop Richard's urgent appeal to Pope Nicholas IV (1288–92) on 18 April 1290 for Thomas's canonisation. Pope Nicholas responded only with an indulgence of a year and 40 days, for anyone who visited Hereford Cathedral on one of four specific feast days and donated money.[38] The impact from episcopal and papal support was certainly felt at Hereford, however. This is shown in the fabric rolls for 1290 to 1291 (the only ones to survive from this period) which record the income at St Thomas's tomb as £178 10s 7d out of the year's total income of £286 1s 5d.[39] To put this monetary figure another way, if we were to assume that every pilgrim to St Thomas's tomb donated a penny, then we would expect a minimum of 42,720 pilgrims over the course of the year.

The second irregularity is harder to explain and concerns the lack of miracles reported and recorded between April 1306 to April 1308. The two-year period was incredibly important for St Thomas's cult as it was the culmination of the work of Bishop Richard and the dean and chapter. Letters in Bishop Richard's episcopal register show that 1306 was a year in which his efforts to attain his predecessor's canonisation were at their peak. On 23 April he wrote to the English cardinal, Thomas de Jorz, regarding the appointment of John of Ross as a canon of Hereford Cathedral, and his hopes that John would continue his efforts to promote Thomas de Cantilupe for canonisation at the papal curia where he was resident. Likewise, a similar letter was sent to John, emphasising these hopes.[40] Finally, on 23 August 1306, Bishop Richard's requests for a canonisation inquiry were answered when Pope Clement V (1305–14) issued a papal bull instituting proceedings.[41] Following this, on 15 September 1306, Bishop Richard and the dean and chapter of Hereford Cathedral appointed proctors to make inquiries into local miracles attributed to Thomas and to make reports ready for the canonisation inquiry.[42]

In 1307, the canonisation commissioners appointed by Pope Clement finally began their inquiry. Between 15 April and 15 June 1307 the commissioners undertook an investigation into Thomas's excommunication at the hands of his metropolitan primate, Archbishop John Peckham of Canterbury. They found that Thomas had indeed been absolved by Pope Martin IV (1281–85) before his death and thus the canonisation inquiry officially started.[43] The inquiry began on 13 July 1307 in London and closed on 12 August. It then moved to Hereford on 28 August and continued until 12 November. Should any miracle recipients have come forward between April and November, it would certainly stand to reason that they would have been interviewed by the commissioners on the spot; yet, VL 4015 contains no such testimonies. The only possible explanation is that the cathedral authorities sequestered the shrine-registrars for other, more pressing, duties throughout the period, although this

Year	Blind	Deaf	Mute	Cripple	Mad	Illness	Resurrection	Animal	Maritime	Other	Total people cured
1287–88	32	5	9	84	6	30	—	1	1	7	166
1288–89	—	—	1	6	5	6	12	2	3	1	34
1289–90	1	—	1	2	2	7	7	5	2	4	27
1290–91	1	—	1	2	2	19	6	5	4	—	40
1291–92	1	1	—	4	5	4	3	2	1	2	18
1292–93	2	1	1	3	2	8	2	1	1	—	20
1293–94	1	—	—	1	1	2	2	1	2	2	11
1294–95	1	—	—	1	1	5	4	2	2	2	16
1295–96	—	—	—	1	—	—	1	—	—	1	3
1296–97	2	—	—	3	2	5	3	2	2	3	18
1297–98	—	—	—	—	—	—	—	—	—	—	0
1298–99	1	—	—	—	—	—	—	—	—	—	1
1299–1300	3	—	—	—	1	1	4	1	—	1	8
1300–01	1	1	—	—	1	—	4	1	—	1	9
1301–02	2	—	2	—	—	2	2	—	1	1	8
1302–03	4	—	3	5	—	6	8	1	—	3	19
1303–04	—	—	1	—	—	1	4	1	—	2	8
1304–05	2	—	1	1	—	—	1	—	—	—	4

Year	Blind	Deaf	Mute	Cripple	Mad	Illness	Resurrection	Animal	Maritime	Other	Total people cured
1305–06	—	—	1	2	—	1	1	—	—	—	5
1306–07	—	—	—	—	—	—	—	—	—	—	0
1307–08	—	—	—	—	—	—	—	—	—	—	0
1308–09	—	—	—	—	—	1	1	—	—	—	2
1309–10	1	—	—	1	—	1	1	3	—	—	7
1310–11	1	—	—	1	—	1	2	—	—	—	3
1311–12	—	—	—	1	1	—	1	—	—	—	3
1312	1	1	1	1	—	—	—	—	1	—	1
1404	—	—	—	—	—	—	—	—	1	—	1
Total reported ailments	57	9	22	119	29	100	69	28	20	30	

Table Two: Recorded Miracle Cures in Exeter 158

still does not explain why the gap in miracles continued for as long as it did. As it stands, the lack of miracles performed between April 1306 and April 1308 marks itself out primarily as an unexplainable phenomenon, especially when considering that this was the zenith of promotion efforts with a resulting canonisation inquiry.

In terms of conclusions that we can reach from this breakdown, it can be seen that by the end of the third year of the cult (April 1289 to April 1290) 49.7% of all miraculous cures had been recorded at the shrine. Indeed, from the first month of 1287 onwards there seems to have been a sharp decline in miracle performance, with April 1287 accounting for some 70 miracles, and declining to only two in December that year. On the other hand, while the decline might, at first, seem rather pronounced, when one examines the breakdown, it can be seen that from the second year (April 1288 to April 1289) onwards the cult appears to go through cycles of high and low miracle-performing years. This cycle eventually changes, with 1303 to 1304 marking a new start of high and low years. For some years these fluctuations have probable explanations; for example, letters from the bishops and king of England petition-ing the papacy for Thomas de Cantilupe's canonisation were dis-patched in 1294, 1299 and 1305 – all years corresponding to high miracle yields, and indicating that support in this manner might have coalesced in the form of increased pilgrimage.[44] Aside from this, variances in recorded cures, as shown in Table Two above, seem to conform to years of high miracle output, with different cures becoming more prevalent for different reasons.

Table Two shows the variances in reported ailments, and that the 432 miracle recipients recorded in Exeter 158 reported 483 ailments in total. As can be seen, the highest totals are for those with crippled limbs, resuscitation of the dead and cures from blindness. Several of the reported cures seem to have risen and fallen in prominence too;

for example, in the first year of the cult, crippled limbs were the most prevalent reported cure, then in the second year this shifted to revival from death, and in the third year it was cures from various, often undefined, illnesses. Likewise, it can be seen that during the high miracle years some cures were more prominent than others and there also seems to be a cycle, with ailments rising and falling.

CONCLUSION

This essay has highlighted St Thomas de Cantilupe's placement as Hereford Cathedral's third patron saint by examining some of the miracle stories in which he has appeared alongside his co-patrons, the Virgin Mary and St Ethelbert, as well as highlighting the scope and scale of the extant miracle collection. The collection is a fascinating document to have survived from the Middle Ages, offering a unique glimpse into single events in the daily life of people, which are otherwise not covered in the surviving records. In celebrating the 700th anniversary of St Thomas de Cantilupe's canonisation and his appointment as Hereford Cathedral's third patron saint, we also celebrate the miracles that were attested to at the shrine during the height of the posthumous cult between 1287 and 1312, bearing witness to political upheaval, rebellion, conflict, daily life, illness, pilgrimage and life and death. Although these were not positive experiences for an individual until they received a miracle, Bishops Richard Frith and Richard Jackson in their foreword are right to pick up on the great Christian themes present in both St Thomas's ministry and his miracle collection: those of 'healing, redemption and faithfulness'. As we come to the surviving shrine in the north transept in this anniversary year, we may well each add our own miracle stories to those that were inscribed some 700 years ago, thus continuing a long-standing tradition with St Thomas in his role as intercessor.

NOTES

1 My sincere thanks to the Very Revd Michael Tavinor, dean of Hereford, for inviting me to write this paper for the end of our book to celebrate the 700th anniversary of the canonisation of St Thomas of Hereford. Also my thanks to my parents, Keith and Margaret, for casting critical eyes over the draft, and to Lydia Prosser for providing translations of several miracles.

2 *The Register of Adam de Orleton, Bishop of Hereford (A.D. 1317–1327)*, ed. by A.T. Bannister, Canterbury and York Society 5 (Hereford: Wilson and Phillips, 1907), pp. 143–44. This letter followed one issued to the archbishop of Canterbury and bishops of England on 2 September 1320 requesting they hold a special celebration of St Thomas's first feast day: *Ibid.*, pp. 139–40.

3 *Ibid.*, p. 144. 'Nos enim, de omnipotentis Dei misericordia, gloriose Virginis Marie genetricis ipsius, beati Ethelberti Regis et Martiris, et ejusdem sancti Thome Episcopi et confessoris, patronorum nostrorum, necnon et omnium sanctorum meritis intercessionibus confidentes.'

4 P.E. Morgan, 'The effect of the pilgrim cult of St Thomas Cantilupe on Hereford Cathedral', in *St Thomas Cantilupe, Bishop of Hereford: Essays in his Honour* (Hereford: The Friends of Hereford Cathedral Publications, 1982), pp. 145–53; R. Morris, 'The Remodelling of the Hereford Aisles', *The Journal of the British Archaeological Association*, 3rd ser. 37 (1974), 21–39; *Idem*, 'The Architectural History of the Medieval Church', in *Hereford Cathedral: A History*, ed. by Gerald Aylmer and John Tiller (London and Rio Grande: The Hambledon Press, 2000), pp. 203–40, at pp. 218–24; Phillip Lindley, 'Retrospective Effigies, the Past and Lies', in *Hereford: Medieval Art, Architecture and Archaeology*, ed. by David Whitehead, British Archaeological Association Conference Transactions 15 (Leeds: W.S. Maney and Son Ltd, 1995), pp. 111–21.

5 Oxford, Exeter College, MS 158, fol. 1r. For John de Massington's role as forester at Bosbury: Hereford, Herefordshire Archives and Records Centre, AA59/A/1, fol. 33r; A.T. Bannister, 'A Transcript of "The Red Book" of the Bishopric of Hereford (*c*.1290)', in *Camden Miscellany*, xv (London: Offices of the Camden Society, 1929), i–ix, 1–36, at p. 18.

6 For surveys of the manuscript evidence see: Patrick H. Daly, 'Thomas de Cantilupe, bishop of Hereford, *c*.1222–1282: the making of a medieval saint', 2 vols (unpublished doctoral thesis, Katholeike Universiteit Leuven, 1981), i, pp. 35–52; Harriett Webster, 'Mediating memory: recalling and recording miracles of St Thomas Cantilupe', in *Power, Identity and Miracles on a Medieval Frontier*, ed. by Catherine A.M. Clarke (London: Routledge, 2016), pp. 44–60, originally published in *Journal of Medieval History*, 41 (2015), 292–308; Ian L. Bass, 'St Thomas de Cantilupe's Welsh Miracles', *Studia Celtica*, 53 (2019), 83–102, at pp. 83–86.

7 *Nova Legenda Anglie: Collected by John of Tynemouth, John Capgrave, and others*, ed. by Carl Horstman, 2 vols (Oxford: The Clarendon Press, 1901), ii, pp. 372–73.

8 Oxford, Exeter College, MS 158. Following conventions established in previous articles, the Oxford manuscript will be abbreviated as Exeter 158 throughout. The manuscript is available for consultation in microfilm format at Hereford Cathedral too, and it is from this microfilm that this essay has been produced.

9 A full copy of the *relatio processus* text survives in Paris, Bibliothéque Nationale de France, 5373A, fo. 66r–69v; Rome, Bibliotheca Alexandrina, Cod. 99, fo. 751–805r. See André Vauchez, *Sainthood in the Later Middle Ages*, trans. by Jean Birrell (Cambridge: Cambridge University Press, 1997), pp. 540–54 for a transcription of the Paris *relatio processus*; also, for a recent examination see Stefan Dragulinescu, 'Thomas of Hereford's miracles – between Aquinas and Augustine', *Journal of Medieval History*, 44/5 (2018), 543–68.

10 Vatican, Biblioteca Apostolica Vaticana, Vat. Cod. Lat. 4015. Following conventions established in previous articles the Vatican manuscript will be abbreviated as VL4015 throughout. It is the author's understanding that Professor Susan Ridyard is still in the process of producing an edition of VL 4015 for the Oxford Medieval Texts series. The manuscript is available for consultation in microfilm format at Hereford Cathedral too. VL 4015 has recently been digitised: DigiVatLib, *Manuscript – Vat.lat.4015* <https://digi.vatlib.it/view/MSS_Vat.lat.4015> [accessed 01 March 2020].

11 Ronald C. Finucane, *Miracles and Pilgrims: Popular Beliefs in Medieval England*, rev. ed. (New York: St. Martin's Press, 1977), p. 173.

12 Robert Bartlett, *The Hanged Man: A Story of Miracle, Memory and Colonialism in the Middle Ages* (Princeton: Princeton University Press, 2004); *The Saint and the Hanged Man*, BBC Four, 1 episode, 16 April 2008, 9:00p.m.; City Witness, *Medieval Swansea*, <http://www.medievalswansea.ac.uk/en/> [accessed 01 March 2020]; St Thomas Way, <http://thomasway.ac.uk/> [accessed 01 March 2020]. There is an extensive bibliography around the Cragh miracle, see: Ian L. Bass, 'Rebellion and Miracles on the Welsh March: Accounts in the Miracle Collection of St Thomas de Cantilupe', *The Welsh History Review*, 29/4 (2019), 503–31, at pp. 504–05 nn. 3–4. The Swansea City Witness project also released a series of academic articles, *Power, Identity and Miracles*, ed. by Clarke (see no. 6 above). A similar monograph is available for the St Thomas Way: *The St. Thomas Way and the Medieval March of Wales: Exploring Place, Heritage, Pilgrimage*, ed. by Catherine A.M. Clarke, Medieval Places and Spaces 1 (Amsterdam: Amsterdam University Press and Arc Humanities Press, 2020).

13 *The Register of Richard de Swinfield, Bishop of Hereford (A.D. 1283–1317)*, ed. by W.W. Capes, Canterbury and York Society 6 (Hereford: Wilson and Phillips, 1909), p. 68. For the miraculous spring: *Annales Prioratus de Wigornia (A.D. 1–1377)*, in *Annales Monastici*, ed. by Henry Richards Luard, 5 vols, Rolls Series 36 (London: Longman, Green, Longman, Roberts and Green, 1864–69), IV, p. 483.

14 For further examinations of this miracle see: R.C. Finucane, 'Cantilupe as Thaumaturge: Pilgrims and their Miracles', in *St Thomas Cantilupe*, ed. by Jancey, pp. 137–44; Michael Goodich, 'Microhistory and the inquisitiones into the life and miracles of Philip of Bourges and Thomas of Hereford', in *Medieval Narrative Sources: A Gateway into the Medieval Mind*, ed. by Wener Verbeke, Ludo Milis and Jean Goossens, Mediaevalia Lovaniensia 34 (Leuven: Leuven University Press, 2005), pp. 91–106, at pp. 99–106.

15 VL 4015, fol. 211v–212r.

16 VL 4015, fol. 211r.

17 R.C. Finucane, 'The Cantilupe-Pecham controversy', in *St Thomas Cantilupe*, ed. Jancey, pp. 103–24, at pp. 122–23.

18 Exeter 158, fol. 21v; VL 4015, fol. 289r.

19 Exeter 158, fols 49v–51v; Vauchez, *Sainthood*, pp. 542–44.

20 Exeter 158, fol. 7v.

21 See Ian Bass, 'Miraculous Marches: The Cult of Thomas de Cantilupe and the Mortimers', *The Journal of the Mortimer History Society*, 1 (2018), 1–18, at pp. 15–16.

22 VL 4015, fols 125v–126r. '*Et cum aliquantulum dicta puella resumpsisset vires circa ortum solis portaverunt eam ad ecclesiam parochialem dicti loci et posuerunt eam altare sancti Ethelberti regis et martiris patroni ecclesie Herefordiensis.*'

23 VL 4015, fol. 123v. '*Communiter et publice in dicta parochia vocant eam virginem sancti Thome.*'

24 Michael Tavinor, *Ethelbert, King & Martyr: Hereford's Patron Saint* (Eardisley: Logaston Press, 2018), p. 1.

25 Exeter 158, fols 26v–27r; VL 4015, fol. 293v.

26 There are collections of miracles for the Virgin too: William of Malmesbury, *The Miracles of the Blessed Virgin Mary*, ed. and trans. by R.M. Thomson and M. Winterbottom, Boydell Medieval Texts (Woodbridge: The Boydell Press, 2015).

27 Exeter 158, fols 20v–21r; VL 4015, fol. 288r.

28 Exeter 158, fols 25v–26r; VL 4015, fol. 293r–v. '*vade ad tumulum Sancte Thome que est Herefordie et ibidem optatam recipies sanitatem.*'

29 See also, Ian L. Bass, 'Communities of Remembrance: Religious Orders and the Cult of Thomas de Cantilupe, bishop of Hereford (1275–82)', *The Journal of Medieval Monastic Studies*, 7 (2018), 236–72, at pp. 254–55.

30 For comparisons see: Anne J. Duggan, 'The Cult of St Thomas Becket in the Thirteenth Century', in *St Thomas Cantilupe*, ed. by Jancey, pp. 21–44; Ian L. Bass, 'England's Two Thomases: Episcopal Models of Sanctity Embodied in Thomas Becket and Thomas de Cantilupe', in *Episcopal Power and Personality in Medieval Europe, 900–1480*, ed. by Peter Coss, Chris Dennis, Melissa Julian-Jones and Angelo Silvestri, Medieval Church Studies 42 (Turnhout: Brepols, 2020), pp. 141–61. A forthcoming article further explores iconographical associations of England's Two Thomases: Ian L. Bass, 'Reflected Glory? An examination of the mitred bishop on the east splay of the south window of St Mary's Church, Kempley (Gloucestershire)'. For the 'Becketization' of medieval English cult centres see: John Jenkins, 'Replication or Rivalry? The "Becketization" of Pilgrimage in English Cathedrals', *Religion*, 49 (2019), 24–47.

31 *The Hereford Breviary, Edited from the Rouen Edition of 1505*, ed. by Walter Howard Frere and Langton E.G. Brown, 3 vols (London: Henry Bradshaw Society, 1904–13), II, p. 349.

32 Virginia C. Raguin and Naomi Reed Kline, 'Relics and the two Thomases: Thomas of Canterbury and Thomas of Hereford as bishop martyr and bishop confessor', in *Catholic Collecting: Catholic Reflection, 1538–1850*, ed. by Virginia C. Raguin (Worcester Massachusetts: The Catholic University of America Press, 2006), pp. 69–78, at p. 75.

33 Oxford, Bodleian Library, MS Gen, Top. D.13, fol. 17; Thomas Dingley, *History from Marble, compiled in the reign of Charles II*, 2 vols (London: Camden Society, 1867), II, p. 189 (foliated clxxxix).

34 Dingley, *History from Marble*, II, p. 140 (foliated clxxviii). The funerary monument of Peter, Lord Grandison (*d.1358*) survives with images of St Thomas Becket, St Ethelbert, the Virgin Mary and Christ, St John the Baptist and St Thomas Cantilupe, as does the funerary brass of Archdeacon Richard Rudhale (*d.1476*) with its images of St Thomas Cantilupe and St Thomas Becket with other saints. The fourteenth-century window with St Thomas of Canterbury survives in the south-east transept and was restored in 1864. The window with St Thomas of Hereford does not survive, but was located in the south transept, above the tomb of Bishop John Trefnant (1389–1404).

35 This section is based on a longer paper forthcoming in 2020: Ian L. Bass, 'Bishop Cantilupe is Dead! Long Live St Thomas of Hereford! St Thomas of Hereford's Miraculous Cult', *History: Journal of the Historical Association*, special edition edited by Paul Webster and Louise Wilkinson. It is with the kind permission and agreement of Dr Webster and Professor Wilkinson that some conclusions and two tables from the forthcoming paper have been included here.

36 For another statistical study see: R.C. Finucane, 'Pilgrimage in daily life: Aspects of medieval communication reflected in the newly-established cult of Thomas de Cantilupe (*d.1282*), its dissemination and effects upon outlying Herefordshire villagers', in *Walfahrt und Alltag in Mittelalter und Früher Neuzeit*, ed. by Gerhard Jaritz and Barbara Schuh (Wein: Verlag de Österreichischen Akademie der Wissenschaften, 1992), pp. 165–218.

37 *Councils & Synods with other documents relating to the English Church*, ed. by F.M. Powicke and C.R. Cheney and others, 2 vols in 4 parts (Oxford: The Clarendon Press, 1964–81), II/2, p. 1090; Finucane, 'Pilgrimage', p. 197.

38 *The Register of Richard de Swinfield*, ed. by Capes, pp. 234–35; W.H. Bliss and others, *Calendar of Entries in the Papal Registers Relating to Great Britain and Ireland*, 16 vols (London: HMSO, 1893–1989), I, p. 521.

39 Hereford, Hereford Cathedral Archives, 2368; see also W. Nigel Yates, 'The fabric rolls of Hereford Cathedral 1290/1 and 1386/7', *National Library of Wales Journal*, 18 (1973), pp. 79–86; Morgan, 'The effect of the pilgrim cult', p. 147.

40 *The Register of Richard de Swinfield*, ed. by Capes, pp. 428–29.

41 Hereford, Hereford Cathedral Archives, 1441; VL 4015, fols 2r–3r; also in: *Registrum Simonis de Gandavo, diocesis saresbiriensis A.D. 1297–1315*, ed. by C.T. Flower and M.C.B. Dawes, 2 vols, Canterbury and York Society 40 and 41 (Oxford: For the Society, 1934), I, pp. 247–48, 249–52; *Annales Londonienses*, in *Chronicles of the Reigns of Edward I and Edward II*, ed. by William Stubbs, 2 vols, Rolls Series 76 (London: Longman & Co., 1882–83), I, p. 150.

42 *The Register of Richard de Swinfield*, ed. by Capes, p. 430.

43 Vatican, Biblioteca Apostolica Vaticana, Vat. Cod. Lat. 4016.

44 VL 4015, fols 262v–265r; Patrick H. Daly, 'The process of canonization in the thirteenth and early fourteenth centuries', in *St Thomas Cantilupe*, ed. by Jancey, pp. 125–34, at pp. 127–28. For the proforma that was sent out by Bishop Richard see, *The Register of Richard de Swinfield*, ed. by Capes, pp. 420–21, 440–41.

45 A similar table was compiled by John M. Theilmann, 'English peasants and medieval miracle lists', *The Historian*, 52/2 (1990), 286–303, at p. 292, though this contains more specific breakdowns of illnesses.

• • •